TRUE SELVES

Hazelden Titles of Related Interest

JourneyNotes: Writing for Recovery and Spiritual Growth,
Roseann Lloyd and Richard Solly

Catching Fire: Men Coming Alive in Recovery, Merle Fossum

Codependent No More, Melody Beattie

Beyond Codependency, Melody Beattie

The Language of Letting Go, Melody Beattie

TRUE SELVES:
Twelve Step Recovery
From Codependency

Roseann Lloyd and Merle Fossum

Photographs by Tony Nelson and Terry Gydesen

A Hazelden Book
HarperCollins*Publishers*

FIRST HARPERCOLLINS EDITION PUBLISHED IN 1991.

Library of Congress Cataloging-in-Publication Data

Lloyd, Roseann.
    True selves: twelve-step recovery from codependency / Roseann
Lloyd and Merle Fossum.—1st HarperCollins ed.
      p. cm.
"A Hazelden book"
ISBN 0-06-255335-6
  1. Codependents—Rehabilitation.   2. Twelve-step programs.
I. Fossum, Merle A.   II. Title
RC569.5.C63L57   1991
616.86—dc20
                                             91–55084
                                                     CIP

---

91 92 93 94 95 MAL 10 9 8 7 6 5 4 3 2 1

This edition is printed on acid-free paper that meets the American National Standards Institute Z39.48 Standard.

To all people in recovery
who are finding
their true selves as
they tell their stories.

Contents

Acknowledgments

We thank the writers, editors, and publishers who granted us permission to reprint the following poems:

Berry, Wendell, "The Peace of Wild Things" from OPENINGS, copyright © 1968 by Wendell Berry. Reprinted by permission of Harcourt Brace Jovanovich, inc.

Levertov, Denise: *A Door in the Hive.* Copyright © 1989 by Denise Levertov. Reprinted by permission of New Directions Publishing Corporation.

Moore, Jim, "Today's Meditation: Happiness" from *The Freedom of History,* copyright © 1989 by Jim Moore. Reprinted by permission of Milkweed Editions.

Oliver, Mary, "Wild Geese," from DREAM WORK by Mary Oliver. Copyright © 1986 by Mary Oliver. Used by permission of Atlantic Monthly Press.

The following publishers have generously given permission to reprint the Twelve Steps: From *Alcoholics Anonymous,* copyright © 1976, by A.A. World Services, Inc. The Twelve Steps are reprinted and adapted with permission of Alcoholics Anonymous World Services, Inc. Permission to reprint and adapt the Twelve Steps does not mean that AA has reviewed or approved the contents of this publication, nor that AA agrees with the views expressed herein. The views expressed herein are solely those of the authors. AA is a program of recovery from alcoholism—use of the Twelve Steps in connection with programs and activities which are patterned after AA, but which address other problems, does not imply otherwise. From *Al-Anon Faces Alcoholism,* copyright © 1986, by Al-Anon Family Group Headquarters, Inc. Reprinted by permission of Al-Anon Family Group Headquarters, Inc.

The following publisher has given permission to reprint the First and Second Tradition of Al-Anon: From *Al-Anon's Twelve Steps and Twelve Traditions,* copyright © 1981, by Al-Anon Family Group Headquarters, Inc. Reprinted by permission of Al-Anon Family Group Headquarters, Inc.

Introduction

There are no final answers to life's questions. We seek a way to live that offers continuing renewal rather than a once-and-for-all-time cure.

We present you this book as a practical guide to the Twelve Steps and a path to the discovery and development of your true self. The Steps provide a framework to give shape and direction to the many facets of your growth. As we wrote the book, we had in mind those who may have just started in a Twelve Step group and were looking for answers to questions like *How should I take these Steps?* We also had in mind those who have been on a recovery path for a long time and now seek to revitalize it. The book is down-to-earth to help you plant your feet firmly in the practical world; at the same time it is designed to nurture and fill your soul and let your spirit soar.

As coauthors, we first met when we began planning this book. We had no idea about how we would get along or how well we would work together. Over the months, our work turned out to be a spiritual experience in the way that a good meeting is. We always met at restaurants where the management didn't mind writers who sprawled their papers across a booth and settled in for some work. Through many cups of coffee, the subject of the book led us to tell our own life stories to each other, illustrate lessons we still live by, and exchange the best of what we have learned. We revealed dark and painful times and the wisdom that others taught us on our journeys; we laughed at silly situations and human imperfections in our lives. After each work session we left with the feeling that we had been personally enriched.

Thank you to our editor, Rebecca Post, for initiating and encouraging us in writing this book, for her grace and patience when painful circumstances forced delays, and for her fine act of selecting two people who could work so well together.

We have adapted the Twelve Steps based on the Steps used by Al-Anon and Co-Dependents Anonymous (CoDA). In addition, we chose to use lower-case letters for the words *god* and *higher power.* We do so because the Twelve Step program teaches belief in god as you understand god. It does not endorse or support any specific religion. The program is inclusive, spreading an umbrella over many spiritual and religious beliefs. One person may have a very personal relationship with a specific higher power named *God*. Another person has a relationship with a more diffuse god that she or he calls nature, or perhaps the energy of creation. By using lower-case letters we affirm the many varieties of spiritual and religious experience, imposing no definition, no gender identity, and no specific characteristics whatsoever upon any individual's spiritual understanding. At the same time, we believe in the profound value of pursuing those traditions and beliefs that may be more specified and defined than the spirituality of the Twelve Steps.

We also wanted the stories we told in the book to reflect a gender balance. It's a difficult and cumbersome problem to maintain balance in the English language. In our stories and use of pronouns, we've tried various solutions to achieve this important goal.

The case examples in this book are composites of many people with codependency issues. We gave our attention to stories we heard more than once and created typical illustrations from them. No story actually represents any real person that we know. We wish to carefully protect everyone's privacy and anonymity. Any similarity of our examples to specific individuals is coincidental.

SECTION ONE:

THE PROMISE OF CHANGE

I enjoy the pleasures of daily life.

CHAPTER ONE

*Your problems are signs to me
of a valiant attempt to cope with
extreme circumstances.*
—Virginia Satir

Codependency:
Living for the Eyes of Others

A ny person who ever lived with an alcoholic or other addict was forever changed by the experience. Children, partners, brothers, sisters, and parents all have their stories to tell. Partners know the growing confusion that comes with the roller coaster ride of personality changes. Adults recall childhood feelings of abandonment and fear. Brothers and sisters tell about the craziness of life when their families turned all concern and attention toward the behavior problems of one chemically dependent sibling.

Experiences Change Us

Living organisms must respond. We respond to what happens around us because we are alive. We cannot *not* respond. People become human through their emotional bonds with other people. When we are attached to people who are abusive, compulsive, addictive, or self-destructive, our own development also gets skewed. Each of the family members mentioned above was forced to respond, and their responses changed them in turn. They had to learn how to cope with abnormal circumstances. They changed not just because of one or two events that demanded responses, but because of many of them.

If your father raises your hopes, promising you a bicycle for your birthday, and then doesn't even come home on your special day until long past your bedtime (and empty-handed at that), you will add it to all the other unpredictable responses from him. Eventually you learn not to rely on the promises of people close to you.

Perhaps you never know when you come home after school whether your mother will be competent or in her intoxicated world. Then you may learn more skills for coping with unpredictability than for being in a close and trusting relationship.

Perhaps your father is usually distant but periodically gets drunk, and then his tongue loosens to talk about his feelings. You feel you get past his wall, but then he only shows sadness, regret, and self-pity. Your childlike mind develops great pity for him and you are glad to get close to him by taking care of his needs. So you develop a role reversal, the child playing the parent's role in order to find a place.

For some families, addiction progresses quickly, like wildfire, into chaos and family disarray. For others the progression is slow. Children see their youthful parents gradually, almost imperceptibly, become slaves to a chemical addiction or a behavior. The child gets shunted into a secondary place. With no announcements—and probably no acknowledgment—reality changes. The family changes. Whether it happens quickly or gradually, the child is robbed of a reliable, engaged parent and instead gets one who is emotionally absent—either drunk or distracted because of his or her own personal struggle.

Children, spouses, siblings, parents, employees, friends, or anyone in a close relationship with a victim of addiction becomes a victim of the addiction as well. They develop a pattern of common characteristics called *codependency*. This pattern is made up of coping responses, feelings, and emotional scars that encourage a person to build up a false self.

We see the pattern in families in which a member has an addiction. We also see it in families troubled by chronic illness or physical, emotional, or sexual abuse. It often gets passed through several generations. Parents who are not themselves addicted but were raised by an abusive or addicted parent may unintentionally pass along the pattern.

We are talking about a pattern of coping responses, feelings, and emotional scars that is largely invisible to those within its grip. Learning to see its shape and design empowers people, gives them new options, and points to their release from the false self and its stifling confusion and mystification.

Hallmarks of Codependency

One of the hallmarks of the pattern of codependency is an inner feeling of being caught in a double bind. One man described it like this:

> I can't seem to do anything right! My wife wants me to tell her what I feel, but whenever I start to feel down or scared, she outdoes me by getting even more upset than I am. So I get strong again just to keep our family from spinning into a big crisis. Then we're soon back to her criticizing me for not telling her how I feel.

Another way that bind is felt is through pervasive guilt:

> Every time I turn around and every time anything goes wrong I think it must be my fault. Even when I don't think it could possibly be my fault I feel guilty and wonder what I should have done differently.

People in these impossible binds usually don't recognize their bind and can't put their finger on it. They just feel unsuccessful, confused, awkward, stupid, angry, or incapable of doing anything right.

Another hallmark of the codependency pattern is found in people who are totally dedicated to being "good." They may begin with what our culture says a good person is. Starting in childhood with a fierce commitment to being the good girl or the good boy, they seek to learn the rules as soon as possible so they can follow them.

This pattern merges lovableness with propriety: "If I am a good girl (or good boy) I will earn and deserve the love of others." This good child grown into adulthood doesn't feel adult because he or she is simply a good big child. The roles of adulthood become stereotypes; grown men just strive harder to be good husbands, good fathers, good breadwinners, while grown women strive harder to be good wives, good moms, good nurturers. But these are just roles to play, a script or a set of rules. These people may be virtuous and laudable in their roles, but their personal

7

development is still incomplete. Fulfilling a role creates the part of a self that follows external rules, but it doesn't develop a grown-up, wholesome inner self.

Self-control was mistakenly thought of as the answer to shaping oneself as a good person. But in codependency, control is the problem. The good-person role, like any overdeveloped role, becomes a painful trap for the person trying to fill it.

Another hallmark is in the person who is a "good coper." This is the resourceful person who is always the central pillar of strength in the midst of chaos. Here we find the sainted, patient wife or the heroic, problem-solving husband, the one who has been confronted with an unbelievable amount of trouble or misbehavior by a spouse or child and always finds a way to fix it, tolerate it, get beyond it, and go forward. Strength in coping with crisis is admirable, even heroic, but when people are caught in this pattern they don't see that they have a self with value. They don't see that they have an option to say, "I have reached my limit. I will not meet your unacceptable behavior with patience and resourcefulness forever!"

Origins of the Concept of Codependency

In the late 1950s and 1960s a few psychotherapists—the original family therapists—developed a new insight. They said that psychological problems exist *between* people in their patterns of verbal and nonverbal communication, not just *inside* individuals. When chemical dependency counselors met family therapists, they began to include whole families in the treatment of chemical dependency rather than simply trying to help one individual to change alone.

Treating whole families made obvious what was previously hidden: addiction doesn't take root and grow in individuals apart from their surroundings. It was suddenly more clear that whole families became organized around a chemical or a behavior. Their best intentions became twisted and distorted into self-defeating coping behaviors, even when only one of them was an addict, and even if the addict belonged to a previous generation.

The word *codependency* did not arise from theory or from abstract, ivory-tower reasoning about addiction. It came from the frontline experience of therapists and counselors who saw patterns of behavior among the families they worked with and tried to give words to the patterns.

Even predating the awareness of clinicians, the wives of the early founders of Alcoholics Anonymous in the 1940s got together and recognized that they too had a need for recovery. They had no word like *codependence*. But these wives, out of their own wisdom, formed their own self-help recovery group and named it Al-Anon.

Struggling with Definitions

Codependency has still not been well-defined in satisfactory, logical terms. In her best-selling book, *Codependent No More*, Melody Beattie defines a codependent person as "one who has let another person's behavior affect him or her, and who is obsessed with controlling that person's behavior."[1] Anne Wilson Schaef, in her book *Co-Dependence: Misunderstood—Mistreated*, reviews the definitions of several therapists and writers on codependency, some of whom call it a disease, some of whom say it is a consequence of an addictive substance that distorts a relationship, and others who say it is a condition that exists prior to the development of alcoholism or addiction. Wilson Schaef takes the position that "co-dependence is, indeed, a *disease* that has many forms and that grows out of [an underlying] disease process that is inherent in the [social] system in which we live." She says she believes the underlying disease process gives birth to both addiction and codependency.[2]

Codependency is not a diagnosis, and maybe the word will never be sharply defined. Yet it points to something real for those who have been in a close relationship with an addict and for those who have worked as therapists with families suffering from addiction, chronic illness, shame, or abuse. Most important, the idea of codependency has provided empowerment and liberation for thousands of people caught in the wake of those situations. The word arose out of a practical situation and has proven its practical value to those who have tried everything else. We use the word *codependency* as a signpost that points a way out of the trap and toward personal growth.

Objections to the Word *Codependency*

Some critics say that the term is only another way to label people and blame the family victims. These critics say the whole idea simply describes normal, healthy, human coping responses to very difficult circumstances and then uses the description to blame people for their problems. In other instances, they see the finest human qualities of love, care, and sacrifice for others get mislabeled as codependency. They object to the disparagement of what is best in people.

Some say that because the term is not well-defined, it is meaningless jargon. They say its only value is to the marketing people who first get consumers to adopt the label and then sell them recovery literature.[3] Others say that the term is aimed primarily at women and is simply one of many guilt trips laid on them, that it blames women for their own difficulties when the real problems are sexism, oppression, and inequality.[4]

Some critics mistakenly say the idea of codependency removes responsibility from the addict for his or her life. The Twelve Step recovery program begins with simple messages, but its wisdom goes deeper and deeper with practice. It does not ask people to ignore such realities as sexism, racism, and addiction. When people awaken to how codependency has affected their lives, they stop denying the reality of addiction and oppression, and in so doing they don't release others from responsibility for their own behaviors.

On some points we agree with the critics, and on others we disagree. We know that any good thing can be abused. For instance, some reformers would also have us throw out alcohol, sex, sugar, and television because many people abuse them or get addicted. But these things aren't necessarily harmful.

We have seen the concept of codependency misused and exploited by public speakers who sound as if they're trying to convert and persuade everyone to join their new religion. Their appeal offends us because it distorts and exploits a valuable concept. We don't believe everyone is caught in the codependent trap; we don't think of it as a disease but rather as a pattern of behavior that people sometimes fall into.

Codependency is about the profound loss or lack of development of a true self. Recovery is about the awakening, liberation, and empower-

10

ment of a true self. To discredit the whole concept just because it has been exploited and distorted by misguided or power-seeking people would be a great loss. Instead we wish to build on the clarity that has been achieved so far. We can learn from the criticism and then restate and deepen the positive value of the term.

Use and Misuse of Labels

Words have power. Labels can be used to identify situations and create positive changes, or they can be used to exploit and abuse. A word can name what is wrong and painful while pointing in the direction of change and hope. For example, it might be upsetting and frightening to be told that you have high blood pressure, or that your excessive caretaking is hindering your child's development, but the pain of identifying the situation also points to a direction for dealing with it.

On the other hand, a word can be a put-down, a pigeonhole for people. Labels allow us to brush others aside so that we don't have to treat them as we would like to be treated. We may say that he is a "mental case," she is another "liberal," he is a "controlling person." A term may be more disparaging when used to label a person than when used to describe a person's behavior: "You are trouble!" versus "Your actions are causing trouble!" or "You are codependent!" versus "You have codependent behaviors."

A label may give us a warm feeling of belonging to a group: "I'm a Catholic" or "I'm a Red Sox fan." Sometimes we grab a label and wrap ourselves in it because we want words to explain our lives. We get comfort from saying "That's me!" "I'm a rebel," "I'm the scapegoat," "I'm a slow driver."

A word can be a symbol that points to something beyond itself like a sign on a footpath that says "Mt. Wishbone 10 Kilometers." The sign isn't the mountain itself, but it points to something. A word may point to something much greater than we might guess from its definition. The sign on the footpath may be very ordinary but the actual mountain breathtaking. The definition of a word like *democracy* may seem abstract when you read it in the dictionary, but when you witness its impact on the lives of millions, it becomes much more meaningful.

But a word can also deceive us like a street sign that was twisted and points in the wrong direction or was painted over with graffiti and names something that is not even there. For this reason we are careful about how words are used—and misused.

Codependency as a Signpost, Not a Label

We take the labeling issue seriously. Because we see the term *codependency* as a signpost rather than a label, we will not get into an intellectual discussion here or try to sharpen its definition. We know from experience that the word points to something real.

We speak to those whose lives have fallen into disarray and confusion, who have lost or not developed their true selves because they have been under the impact of addiction. We have seen countless men and women emerge from turmoil and confusion because the ideas around codependency pointed them in a new direction. They had experienced the hard times of loving relationships that were stretched too far, or genuine parental love that was interlaced with abandonment or abuse. What they already knew was not leading them out of their difficulties. More of the same actions, no matter how virtuous and how diligent, only led to more of the same outcomes. The ideas of codependency spoke about their situations and pointed to new alternatives that produced hope and real change.

We believe it is a mistake to say that everyone in American culture has codependent behavior and needs to change. On the other hand, we disagree with those critics who discard the whole idea because some people apply it too broadly.

We also think it is not helpful to label and categorize people. People aren't codependent, their behaviors are. They have codependent outlooks or relationships.

Codependency is both a women's issue and a men's issue. Both men and women get lost or sidetracked in their development when addiction distorts their most devoted, most creative, and most human responses. A man's loss of self may appear more characteristically male in style, and a woman's more characteristically female. For instance, a man might become the extremely pleasing, caretaking "good provider" who is completely wrapped up in fixing external situations for others and keeping them happy but who never has enough energy or attention left over to take good care of himself. A woman might become totally devoted to pleasing and caretaking through nurturing the inner needs

12

and feelings of others, watching every subtle change in others' facial expressions and tones of voice, to the exclusion of ever getting to know herself. Both women and men attend codependency groups—many of them mixed-gender, others exclusively for women or for men.

This book focuses on the very practical: the general pattern called codependency, and recovery through the Twelve Steps developed by Alcoholics Anonymous. Instead of calling codependency a disease, we see it the way family therapist Virginia Satir described many forms of emotional distress: Codependency is "a valiant attempt to cope with extreme circumstances."[5]

Many beginners to the recovery program in codependency misunderstand the first message, which is that they have a problem. They translate that message in terms they are familiar with: *If I have a problem, there must be something wrong with me. I must be at fault* or *You're telling me that my spouse's addiction is my fault.* Some critics demonstrate the same misunderstanding when they say victims get blamed in this program, when in fact the first step of the program teaches not only an element of emotional detachment from the problems of others but also acceptance that you are powerless over the forces of addiction.

The Pattern of Codependency

Lacking a concise definition, we will instead describe the pattern that we call codependency.

In codependency a person may take a strength, a virtuous quality, and overdevelop it, extending the trait beyond its stretching point. A good trait used to cope with extreme circumstances may get overdeveloped. "Good" is positive but "too good" is negative. At its extreme, a strength is distorted into brittleness, a virtue into a fault. For example, helpfulness, when overdeveloped, may turn into intrusiveness, disrespect, and manipulation. The overdeveloped desire to be a good son or daughter, a good mother, a good father, a good husband or wife, or a good friend creates a role-bound person when stretched too far. One woman said, "I went through all the right motions and I felt loved only for what I *did*—never as a real person. I never felt loved for who I *was*."

In codependency, your range of personality skills, the data that you notice, and the choices that you see may grow increasingly narrow. You tend to ignore inner messages from yourself about needs, desires, and feelings, but you give careful attention to the facial expressions, voice tones, and words of other people. You may restrict your focus even further, limiting it to only one person who becomes the target of preoccupation or worry. You are developing into a fine art the one part of your personality that can tune in to other people, but other skills needed for a whole self remain unpracticed. You may have worked so hard at tuning in to the feelings and moods of others that you never learned to ask, *What do I feel? What is good for me? What do I need in my life?*

Many people in codependency were forced by extreme circumstances in their past to take responsibility for the happiness, health, comfort, or security of another person. These were not normal family situations. The extreme circumstances were created by such painful things as a mentally or physically handicapped sibling, a mother dying slowly of an illness, a father with alcoholism, or perfectionist parents who taught their children the same life pattern that was taught to them.

Inevitably, everyone faces a human limit—how much one person can do for another. At that limit, no person can secure another's health, happiness, or safety. Then the person who wants to help faces disappointment, feelings of inadequacy, and powerlessness. For our example, let's say a woman rises to the occasion when she meets this limit. She can accept it rather gracefully, perhaps because she had some good models that showed her how to accept her limitations and because her family members support her. She stays involved and hopes that her partner can find a way to help himself (or herself) and to cope with his ultimate limits. But in that crucial, extreme time, if she cannot gracefully accept her limits, if she does not see them, or if she feels she has no right to stop trying, she may defy nature and redouble her efforts to create what the other person needs. Then her pattern is set; the codependent trap is in place.

As her efforts to help get strained, she turns her attention further away from her own needs. She loses contact or hushes her inner voice. She loses touch with herself. The communication link to her private wisdom is interrupted. She doesn't stop needing, thinking, or feeling, but instead enters a kind of spiritual sleep and sustains a profound loss of contact with her inner knowing.

When overdeveloped, this good deed, an essential human value, becomes a narrow, exclusive focus on others and blocks a man (or woman) from ever getting acquainted with what he himself needs. Not being attuned to himself, not attending to what he needs, he cannot be truly responsible for himself. He may get ill because he has not attended to his health, and then others have to care for him. The consequences of his self-sacrifice and inattention to his own needs build up and finally overwhelm him. He may find himself in bankruptcy, divorce, fired from a job, or failed in school. From within his codependent thinking, he is mystified and wonders how this happened to him. All he can see is what he strived so hard to do. By definition, he can't see his inattention to himself.

In her charming, humorous, and touching way, an Al-Anon member wrote this poem about her relationship with her daughter. It shows the touching warmth of a dedicated mother trying to find the difference between fear for her daughter's safety and over-responsibility.

WHAT YOUR FORTUNE COOKIE TELLS YOU:

There Is Yet Time Enough For You to Take a Different Path.

Time to wander down into the kitchen
to make yet another cup of coffee
sit lazily at the table with
your daughter. Next fall she leaves
for college in Seattle and you've
already begun to grieve. Is that why
you cried for hours, undignified
outbursts into the paper napkins
when she still wasn't home at three
that morning? You called Hennepin
Medical Center Emergency Room and heard
the clinical voice say: "No record of a
seventeen-year-old female brought in." The
police officer on duty at Bryant Precinct
Station assured you she'd probably had

too much to drink and gone to a friend's
house to sleep it off. You found yourself
praying she'd *had* too much to drink and
that the friend was not the boy who'd
been hanging around your living room lately
who, even though he was from a good
family, had GED'd out of high school and was
living in a rented room somewhere, *in the
vicinity of,* his mother told you when you
woke *her* up at 3:30, *12th & Hennepin,* but
even though she didn't know the exact address
you drove down there, *into that vicinity,*
in your husband's car which you had to
sneak out of the garage without waking him
because he thought all your worry unnecessary,
telling you earlier from deep under covers
that she'd come home, she always did, and all
your worry would be for nothing. When you
got down there, you found nothing but deserted
liquor store parking lots, all night grocery stores
guarded by empty-eyed clerks. And she did
come home, just like your husband said. Perhaps
when she's left for good, there'll be time enough
for you to take a different path.

—Anonymous

In codependency, what starts as concern for others can become
an escape from yourself under stress. Just as a hit of cocaine takes
you on a chemical escape, living for others becomes a socially
acceptable springboard out of your own sticky, puzzling problems
and emotional pain. Stress and difficulty still trouble your life,
but it's all "out there," where other people's issues catch your attention, not "in here," where you face self-doubt, insecurity, guilt,
or anger. This is what we mean by saying that "virtue distorted
becomes a fault."

People Pleasing

Wanting to please is part of a codependent pattern. For example,
a woman may be so anxious to please others that she doesn't

dare tell her friend anything that her friend might not like. She never expresses a different opinion and becomes dishonest out of niceness.

Crisis Living

Another part of the pattern is seeing crisis as a normal way of life. A natural response to crisis is to rise to the challenge and overcome it, but after the excitement of repeated crises, a person may become dependent on the intensity and the focus that each crisis creates.

The codependent response grasps every challenge that arises and assigns it a high intensity, as if it were not just a challenge or one of the many jobs and pleasures that you give your energies to, but a compelling crisis. The codependent response is to say to oneself, *Now my priorities are clear. My unresolved feelings and issues, my ambivalence, anxiety, guilt, and anger, my ordinary life routines must all be set aside because I must react to this problem.* For people stuck in this pattern, crisis turns this energy on so that they feel alive and strong in a way that they would otherwise never feel.

Life Under Tight Control

Some people in codependency come out of their stressful backgrounds so guilt-ridden and fearful that they welcome a set of rules as a hopeful way to fix their pain. Having an overly strict set of rules to live by may be one of the signposts of codependency. Like other elements of the larger pattern we are describing, this one has the effect of avoiding inner unresolved and ambivalent feelings.

This search might lead to membership in left-wing "politically correct" groups—or right-wing fundamentalist groups. The common factor is dogmatism. When the rule response to life problems takes rules beyond their function as guidelines into moralistic dictums, the rules constrict behavior and thought. They create overcontrolled, perfectionistic, judgmental people and stifle spontaneity.

Self-Blame

Self-blame is also part of the pattern. When people with a codependent outlook get tricked or seduced into a situation,

17

they not only may feel angry or hurt about it, they will also probably take the blame for letting themselves be deceived: *I should not have let this happen. I should have seen it coming.* A more wholesome response is to acknowledge that you are just as vulnerable to a lie as anyone, and that the person who deceived you is responsible for his or her own actions.

The Painful Consequences

Consequences of this codependent pattern run to the extreme. Well-meaning but overextended people get depleted, used up, and are misunderstood. They suffer from fatigue, try to live up to over-inflated, unrealistic images of what they can or should do, and lack the ability to say no to the demands around them. As a result, they defeat themselves: Their impaired judgment causes them to make mistakes any exhausted person might make. They lose rapport with those they love and, ultimately, with themselves.

Who are the people stuck in this pattern? A rising company manager, struggling to do more than anyone could on her job and at home, neglecting her own health until she is struck down by a serious illness. Or a long-suffering, always-dedicated father who knows only how to help his children and never learns how to let go of them, finally reaping more anger and alienation than love and pleasure from their relationship. An employee who gets implicated in criminal activity by covering up his boss's embezzlement. The lover who goes bankrupt because she never could say no to her partner's compulsive spending problem.

The consequences don't always manifest themselves in such dramatic scenarios as jail or bankruptcy: a woman feels that her life is in constant turmoil and stress; a man worries that he always attracts an alcoholic or addicted mate; another man always turns himself inside out to achieve and do what's right, yet still feels his self-worth belongs in a garbage dump.

The Way Out: A More True Self

We think of people in recovery from codependency as seeking a more true self. The false self was a shirt we put on to shield us against the winds of trying circumstances, to protect us from danger and chaos, to look good, to please others. So much attention to others and to outside dangers impeded or blocked development of a true self.

In recovery a new person awakens to his or her authentic self. Such a woman or man starts to feel like a real person, a grown-up, rather than an empty nobody or an insecure child.

People who feel like grown-ups typically notice a natural ebb and flow in their life rhythms. Sometimes they feel more self-confident and other times less so, but they know that they have a right to their feelings, whatever they are. They feel competent to deal with most tasks and challenges in their lives. They can be generous and giving, sometimes setting aside their own satisfactions for others because the situation calls for it. They can also set limits on giving and caring for others so that they don't deplete their own reserves of energy and resources.

Sheila, for example, sometimes is dependent when she is sick, tired, or feeling weak. Sometimes she is a caretaker and sometimes an equal, a peer. She has a spiritual sense of her participation in a large network of human relationships and beyond to the whole of creation. She reflects both humility and dignity; she is honest with herself and open to others. She can be angry, selfish, and dishonest; she can make mistakes and exhibit unattractive qualities and imperfections yet still be patient and self-tolerant. Finally, she never stops learning. Although life continues to be difficult for her at times, she continues to grow stronger and deeper as a human being.

The ideal adult we are describing is beyond what we expect of a child. This description is also too simple to encompass the aliveness and spontaneity of any mature adult. What we want to emphasize is the inner personal power, the variation of feelings, the self-affirming attitude, the relationship with other people and surroundings, and the range of behaviors that a well-rounded person can choose.

Recovery does not mean finally achieving some point of cure or secured happiness. Life is always a struggle. No clear line demarcates codependency from recovery, and no blood test tells you that you have made it. After being stuck in codependent patterns, recovery means getting back into action on a life path toward finding your true self.

I take time to discover myself.
I welcome solitude in my life.

CHAPTER TWO

May my heart flower.
May I know the joy of my own true nature.
May I be healed into this moment.
May I be at peace.
—Stephen Levine

Beginning the Search For Your True Self

Picturing Your Sense of Self

*I*n the first chapter, we talked about codependency as a process that encourages us to develop a false self. It's useful to have a mental picture of your false self. If you can see clearly where you are, you have a stronger chance of seeing what you could become. You will be better able to move beyond your false self, to uncover the real you under the layers and adaptations, and to create new aspects to yourself.

One man says that he's going through the motions and feels like a machine. *What is wrong?* he asks himself. *I did everything that I thought would make me happy, so why isn't my life wonderful?* He might picture his false self as the hollow Tin Man in *The Wizard of Oz.* There is more to him than the working parts of metal.

One woman says that she feels "little." Other people seem bigger, more grown-up than she is. When asked about her false self, she says that she imagines herself sitting at a nursery school table, coloring.

The opposite kind of falseness is true for others—those who feel "bigger than," rather than "less than." One woman who is an overachiever says, "I had a big self-image; I had filled the whole picture with my accomplishments, but it was all done out of insecurity. My public self was very visible, but it was false because it wasn't coming from a whole person." She discovered that

21

she had to do less, take time for relaxation, and start getting acquainted with aspects of herself other than work.

A man says he thinks of himself as stunted. His growth has been thwarted. What picture does the word *stunted* call to mind? Perhaps a crooked tree on the edge of a cliff, bent over by winter storms, yet still surviving. This man wants to do more than survive.

Many people say that they feel invisible. They learned how to fit in so well that they blended in and disappeared. The idea of invisibility is also central to many minority people's description of how they feel in white America. An important book about this idea is *The Invisible Man*, by Ralph Ellison, an African-American writer. Another word to describe this "blending-in" phenomenon is *chameleon*. A chameleon changes colors to fit in with the surroundings. Chameleons know how to survive—but they don't necessarily know their true color.

Other people describe themselves with words that have nothing to do with their outer appearance; rather, they refer to their insides. They may say that they feel empty, that they feel like an empty husk, or that "there's nothing there." Young children have a strong sense of their *insides* and know that there is supposed to be something *there*, indicating that this sensation is with us from an early age.

This sense of emptiness may be expressed in very literal ways. The Norwegian writer Herbjørg Wassmo describes the experience of growing up in an abusive home through her character, the young girl Tora:

> Sit up in bed and be like an empty shell. It felt like her head was swollen up and held that empty shell afloat in the room.[1]

Still others express the sense of falseness in terms of their insides not being real. One woman said, "I did all the things I thought I should do so that I'd get to feel real inside, but I didn't." Children ask whether their stuffed animals have "real insides." This stuffed animal image is a good way to imagine a false self—all that dead cotton batting stuffed in a fake skin to bury the real feelings that humans carry around.

Some people express this sense of emptiness by saying that

they don't exist. Sometimes people who are sexually abused cope with the experience by going out of their bodies; this process is also called *splitting.* They may feel nonexistent even many years later. The term *soul murder* has been used to describe sexual abuse. "Soul murder" is the experience of not existing. As one person explained, "I never knew what people meant by self-esteem, because I had lots of esteem but no self."

When we feel too little, too big, stunted, invisible, stuffed, or empty, we are more vulnerable to the demands of the world—good demands as well as harmful. When we are empty, we are susceptible to others who want to fill us up in any number of invasive and exploitive ways. When we feel unreal, we can easily think that our own needs and wants are not real, and it is easy to give in to other people's needs because they seem so real. Their needs are *realer* than ours.

Once you identify a picture of your false self, let your mind turn that picture into a movie. Imagine a magical process transforming your false self into one that is real and alive:

- Imagine a stuffed rabbit becoming furry and energetic, sniffing around.
- Imagine you being the "right size," neither a child nor a looming giant.
- Imagine an empty shell filling up with thoughts, feelings, plans, memories, likes, and dislikes.
- Imagine a little person growing up, and a stunted tree sending out new green branches.
- Imagine your soul becoming real, being born into existence.
- Imagine an invisible person—you—coming forward into your true colors, with substance, voice, and beauty.
- Imagine yourself as you would like to see yourself—right now.

Affirming Our Right to Change

Change is a frightening process. It's frightening even to acknowledge that we *want* to change, or even that we *might want to begin to think about a change.*

The same powerful forces that encouraged us to become codependent will continue to exist and put pressure on us even as we change. It is important to affirm our right to change as a method of counteracting these pressures. It helps to say, *I have a right to change. I am a beloved child of the universe. I am me, unique and changing. It's okay to be more who I am.*

Boundaries: Learning the Difference Between Me and Not-Me

Everyone who is searching for a truer self faces the issue of *boundaries.* Changing boundaries is unquestionably a crucial part of the recovery from codependency. If you somehow feel smaller, less real, or emptier than the world around you, making the boundaries bigger or different is part of letting yourself grow. The term *boundaries* refers to a person's having a sense of being part of the world, connected to others, yet still separate.

Every person has boundaries. In recovery a person becomes more aware of what boundaries are and makes changes to suit the changing sense of self. In addition, every person who's trying to be healthy has an awareness that boundaries may change according to circumstances. There are private and public boundaries. For example, Charlie had a special nickname, Macko, for his lover, Mike. He used the name affectionately in private and when they were with their friends. But none of their friends used the nickname. Nobody outside of their circle even knew about the nickname. Healthy boundaries mean that some kinds of information sharing, while appropriate between close friends, would not be right between more casual acquaintances.

Like "codependency," *boundaries* is also one of the new buzz words that can be heard everywhere. Just because it is now a fad does not mean that anyone should back off from discussing it. There's always something new that can be learned, even in the heart of a trend.

"Boundaries" is the term often used to describe a changing self-perception. Learning about boundaries includes developing our knowledge of our own needs, wants, and limits. It's also about setting new limits with other people, with work, with our activities. It may also involve setting limits with our inner self—for example, setting a limit on how much time we let ourselves obsess about other people's behaviors.

If you wonder how to begin looking at your boundaries, you might think about the word *balance.* What limits do you need in order to create balance in your life? Time limits, spending limits, or socializing limits? In general, we're always vulnerable to pushing limits. When we push our limits, our lives go out of balance, out of kilter, and we're liable to fall into codependent behaviors, focused as we are on the outside, not our insides.

Sometimes we set new boundaries when we feel our lives are out of balance; other times, boundaries change unconsciously. Still other times, we set boundaries in order to give ourselves more time to be alone. We can change our boundaries at any time. A change in boundaries indicates that changes are taking place in a person's life.

Boundaries Are a Function of Life

Within each human body, there are millions of cells. Each cell has a wall that protects the health of the cell from danger; yet the wall also lets in nutrients. We should be so lucky! We can imagine a city, composed of many cells like a body. The cells cooperate for the good of the whole, yet they are separate. In a healthy community, each person can ward off danger and at the same time receive love and nurturing.

If we continue this comparison of the human community to a human body, we can further see what happens when codependency comes along. One cell plops on another cell, the cell walls break down, and one takes over another. There is no longer separateness. In fact, when this does happen in the human body, it is called a disease. We can imagine this in a simple drawing.

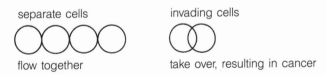

separate cells   invading cells

flow together   take over, resulting in cancer

In order to be psychologically healthy, we need to have boundaries, just as the cells in our bodies need walls. But when we again think of cells, we notice that there are two aspects to having strong cell walls: one is the ability to have definite limits and the other is to let in nutrients to the inside of the cell so that there *is* something inside.

In a similar fashion, current thinking about families stresses the importance of both individuality and togetherness. In fact, these two words are a chapter title in a recent book about families, *Family Evaluation*, by Michael E. Kerr and Murray Bowen. The writers explain that separateness is natural:

> Family systems theory assumes the existence of an instinctually rooted life force . . . in every human being that propels the developing child to grow to be an emotionally separate person. . . .[2]

The writers go on to say that they also assume there is a life force that makes people want to stay connected and experience togetherness. It is inspiring to think of the idea of the life force itself wanting each of us to be separate, to have strong boundaries.

Building Strong Boundaries

If you had to pick an object in the concrete world to represent your boundaries, what would you choose? One woman said her boundaries were mushy, like oatmeal. What about yours? Some people have "mushy" boundaries in some situations and rigid boundaries in others. They may move back and forth between two extremes—runny peanut butter versus peanut brittle. There is danger at both ends of the continuum.

Part of recovery is learning where and when you need to change your boundaries. For example, you may need to set some limits on your volunteer work. You may need to change some relationships. You may decide you cannot spend time with people who are abusive, even though some of these people may be lifelong friends or relatives. You may need to take some time for yourself that you have never taken before, such as an hour alone at a restaurant every Saturday morning.

Learning new boundaries will be a slow process, especially if your boundaries were violated during childhood. Other books deal more extensively with boundary violations. Violations include such actions as *any* unwanted physical contact, invasion of the privacy of your diary, physical abuse, rape, and forced, shaming religious dogma.

As you continue your search, you will learn what you need to do to build new boundaries.

Changing boundaries is a *normal* thing to do. Changing the rules as we go is part of being human. So even though we are saying here that you probably will change some of your boundaries, we think that you can more easily do the work on changing boundaries *after* you have gained a stronger sense of self, the process for which is described in the next section. After you work on giving more to yourself, you will know which boundaries you want to change.

Feeding Your Insides

It's not enough to build strong walls; after all, a wall around an abandoned house is not protecting anything of value. A cell wall in a plant is protecting a living nucleus and other living matter. This cell has the integrity of being a separate entity, a whole unit, even when it is letting in food and making contact. This functioning of cells provides us with the mysterious and hopeful picture of entities that are at once separate and connected.

What can you do to give life to the insides of your cell, your self?

The Gift of Time and Space

Every person exists on the physical level. Do you have a place that is private, only yours, where you can go and relax? Do you let yourself have some time that is not interruptible? One man said that he started going back to church because his life at home was so frantic: "I know that the one thing I can count on at church is that I can sit for an hour with my own thoughts and nobody is going to interrupt me."

The Gift of Physical Health

When we say that we need to feed our insides, we are using food as a metaphor. Yet growing stronger emotionally also involves paying attention to our physical health. In modern life, it seems as though people don't have time to do all the things necessary to be healthy. In fact, many of us feel a twinge of guilt when we look at our diet and sedentary lifestyle. Such simple things as exercise, good food, and sleep, necessary for physical health, also build up emotional well-being and a sense of a separate self.

Taking care of your physical body builds up your sense of self. Taking care of your physical health, whether you are able-bodied or disabled, is *always* integral to your sense of self apart from others.

Recently we heard a courageous story from a young woman who described her process of leaving an abusive marriage to a man who battered her repeatedly. When he started beating her up, she believed that she didn't have the economic resources to leave and care for her children. She didn't have the psychological strength to pack up, protect herself, and get out:

> After hearing the story of another woman on TV who had found the strength to leave, I knew I could do something. I decided that I would do what I could do to get stronger. I decided I could set a deadline to be strong enough to leave within two years. To get stronger, I started walking every day, I started cooking healthy food and stopped eating junk food, and I got a part-time job and started saving money.

This woman did get out within her two-year deadline. Fortunately, she did not suffer lasting physical damage from the domestic violence. She is now living in safety with her children. Of course, if you and your children are in a life-threatening situation, you must do whatever is necessary to ensure your safety.

What is inspiring about her story is how much of her sense of self came from determination to take care of her physical health. It was her starting point, but it is also a continuing necessity. In her plan to be a stronger person, two of the three parts involved physical health. This plan gave her the *self* she needed to leave and find her life.

Like this courageous woman, you can begin today to build up your true self. You can start by giving yourself this gift of physical health: one walk, one bowl of soup.

The Gift of Acknowledgment

No matter how depressed or how hooked on other people's problems you've been, no matter how much you've slaved away for a corporation or family, there is still an individual within you that is *you*. If you don't know this person, you have a wonderful adventure ahead of you! You can start now by getting a notebook and making a list of things you like about yourself. This is a process of acknowledgment. It is an affirmation to see the good qualities you have now. If you're stuck, ask yourself these questions:

- What are the things I actually *do* every day?
- What are my competencies?
- What are some of the things I can do easily?
- What are my favorite things in the world?
- What are some things I do *for myself* that made me feel good about myself?
- What are some of my talents that I'd like to develop later in life?

Finally, give yourself credit for the changes you've made in your life in the last year. These may be small changes, but in recovery, the small changes build. Acknowledge the small changes and you prepare room for bigger changes to happen. A small change might be what we could call the virtue of omission, such as the times you clearly remember *not* nagging, the nights you went to bed and went to sleep rather than worry where your partner was.

Acknowledge who you are now.

The Gift of History
Just as you have unique qualities and competencies, just as you have a unique sense of solitude, you also have a unique history. You feed your insides by acknowledging your history. Your life history may be filled with mistakes and pain and the dullness of following the crowd, yet this history also includes moments of serenity and hope, as well as a vital personality. You need to look back on your life to find your potential true self in your past.

You might look back through photograph albums from your childhood and find one picture from your early life that shows you in a light-hearted mood, at a time when you were in touch with your own free spirit. Take this picture and write about the things you see that you like in this child: playfulness, muscles, energy, a goofy grin, tenderness.

If you grew up in a troubled family, you may have many issues that are interfering with your sense of a personal history. In fact, one common feature of all troubled families is memory loss. You may regain a sense of identity by finding a group that focuses on family issues.

You may not consider yourself a member of an alcoholic or otherwise "labeled" family, and yet you may sense, as did one man: *I don't know what they were but they were something.* This man had no place in his family and was experiencing a sense of disenfranchisement and discounting that was similar to the experience of people in alcoholic families and in minority groups.

To have a history, you need to search for the parts you've lost and reclaim them. You could search by joining a group that deals with inner child and family-of-origin issues. Many Adult Children of Alcoholics (ACOA or ACA) groups assist people in reclaiming the lost qualities of the vital children they once were. This kind of work can help a person who has been disenfranchised for any reason. You can also look for books and movies about people who grew up in situations similar to yours.

No matter how *blank* you feel on the subject of childhood, you first need to believe that it is possible for you to find some history that you can begin to reclaim as yours. You will create your own history by searching for it.

If you are part of a group that has been oppressed in American culture, if you are a person of color, a woman, a Jew or member of another minority religion, a lesbian or gay man, you may have absorbed some of the prejudices of the larger community. Racism, sexism, and homophobia take a toll on people both outwardly and inwardly. If you have taken in other people's prejudices, you may have translated this feeling into self-hatred. One way to release this self-hatred and build a stronger sense of self-worth is to set out to learn about the history of your group, the richness of your history. Some people learn to value their group by talking about prejudice and oppression and by seeking out people with a similar history and outlook. Others find therapists to help release the negative consequences of oppression. Still others begin to study the history of their own culture.

Sometimes parents who are members of an oppressed group withhold important information about history from their children with the good intention of sparing them pain. This silence causes emotional harm to children, and it may last a lifetime unless the grownup children learn to fill in the silence with their true history. Alice Miller has worked with the children of Jews who survived the Holocaust and has written lovingly of the process of reclaiming their identity in her book *Thou Shalt Not Be Aware: Society's Betrayal of the Child.*

Part of recovery work is learning your own individual and group history and appreciating the positive values of your own cultural background. There are many wonderful contemporary writers today who affirm their unique, separate culture within the American culture. For example, the Chicana writer Gloria Anzaldúa writes in *Borderlands/La Frontera* of growing up in Texas, where her family faced prejudice because of color and language.

> I am possessed by a vision: that we Chicanas and
> Chicanos have taken back or uncovered our true faces,
> our dignity and self-respect. It's a validation vision.[3]

The acceptance of *true faces* is a symbol of self-acceptance. The idea of a face is the idea of visibility. It is also a primal idea of self-acceptance: your face is what goes out first into the world; your mother's face was one of the first images you were imprinted with when you were born.

The idea of accepting our faces comes up often. During the time we were writing this book, the U.S. Congress voted to make reparations to the Japanese-Americans who were forced into prison camps during World War II. The law says, "On behalf of the nation, the Congress apologizes." The writer Gene Oishi wrote of the acknowledgment in a recent newspaper article:

> My children and grandchildren are Americans. . . .
> The government of the United States has officially acknowledged that they—*with their Asian faces*—are fully American. . . (emphasis added).[4]

We must all learn to accept the beautiful diversity of the people of this country. We must learn to value our own faces and the faces of others. Our faces carry our histories and bear the traces of our ancestors in a genetic code that cannot be duplicated. Each person has a unique history waiting to be claimed.

The Gift of Self-Awareness

As you begin to pay attention to your self, your history, your feelings, your abilities, your needs, and your physical health, you will also begin to notice your self as it is at any particular moment. You can say, *At this moment I am a unique person, with my own feelings, history, and desires.* Or you may emphasize your ability to survive, as the character Celie does in *The Color Purple*:

"I'm pore, I'm black, I may be ugly and can't cook, a voice say to everything listening. But I'm here."[5]

Like Celie, you are here. You have a self and it is here. What this means in practical terms is that you will learn to value your experience as it is happening. You will be more able to pay attention to your guts, to your thoughts, and decide for yourself what is going on with you. Being present to yourself happens on physical, emotional, spiritual, and intellectual levels.

Paradoxically, being present to yourself gives you a freedom from your history. You won't have to automatically respond as you have always responded in the past. Claiming history liberates you from that history. As you work on building a stronger sense of your self, your own self-worth, you will be free to choose your life. You will be able to live in the present, in the *here and now,* with love for yourself and those other people you choose to love.

The Gift of Connections

Perhaps one of the saddest facts of codependency is that a person can always be "doing" for others and still feel lonely. Sometimes serving others is so draining that there is nothing left.

To combat the feeling of loneliness and emptiness, you need to make emotional connections with people who love you the way you are, and spiritual connections with the world around you. Recovery includes feeling part of a larger whole.

You begin this process of connecting by reclaiming the strengths of your history, by searching through your childhood and your culture to find your missing pieces. All of this work leads to connections, and the stronger your sense of spiritual connection, the stronger your sense of self will be.

Your first task in discovering this gift is setting aside the time to be with others who are on the journey and to develop your spirituality. You need to ask yourself if you're spending time with people who like you the way you are.

You could start by scheduling an hour a week for going to a support group or seeing a friend who is on the same journey.

You might continue by actually writing in time on your calendar—fifteen minutes every day—for meditation on the universe. (Americans always want to comprehend the mystery

of life quickly—fifteen minutes is a pretty long time segment.)
You might meditate by traditional methods or by reading, walking outside, listening to music, dancing.

You could start a list of images that give you a sense of one-
ness with the universe: stars, webs, magnetic fields, the roots
of mushrooms, phone wires.

You could look in poetry books and sacred books for more
images of connection. All of these can be sources of strength.

Spending time outdoors is crucial for many in recovery. Somehow the experience of beauty and awe in nature gives us a sense
of the spirit and of being loved and lovable. A poem by Denise
Levertov may remind us of both walking in the woods and of
the universe:

WEB

Intricate and untraceable
weaving and interweaving,
dark strand with light:

designed, beyond
all spiderly contrivance
to link, not to entrap:

elation, grief, joy, contrition, entwined;
shaking, changing,
                    forever
                            forming,
                                    transforming:
all praise,
        all praise to the
                great web.

SECTION TWO:

HOW THE STEPS WORK

*The connection I have with certain
trustworthy people gives me hope.*

CHAPTER THREE

At the very point of the vulnerability is where the
surrender takes place—that is where the god enters.
The god comes through the wound.
—Marion Woodman

A Light at the End of the Tunnel: Facing Your Problem And Asking for Help

Step One: *We admitted we were powerless over others—that our lives*
             had become unmanageable.[1]

Step Two: *Came to believe that a power greater than ourselves could*
             restore us to sanity.

Step Three: *Made a decision to turn our will and our lives over to*
             the care of god as we understood god.[2]

One way you can intentionally set out to make changes in
your life is to join a Twelve Step program. In the following chapters we will look at each Step and how you can
apply it in your life.

This chapter gets you started on the first three Steps. The opening quotation brings all three Steps together in one idea. The First
Step is like a painful wound. The Second and Third Steps are
the beginning of hope and the flow of help from a source that
Woodman calls "god."[3] You admit that you are facing a situation
beyond your control. That admission can place you on spiritual
ground and make you more accessible to the healing forces from
outside yourself.

*Step One: We admitted we were powerless over alcohol—
that our lives had become unmanageable.*[4]

An ancient Eastern saying: You can't pour more liquid into a
cup that is already full. With the First Step—by admitting your
problem—you pour something out of your cup. You admit that
your own answers haven't worked—that they aren't enough. Now
an empty feeling may arise in you. When you admit that your
best attempts, your most virtuous efforts, haven't worked, you feel
let down. Perhaps you will feel at loose ends in a way you never
felt before. You may feel wounded, broken, vulnerable, defeated.
One person explains the uncertainty: "I feel like I'm walking on
rubber legs since I started in this program. I'm unsure of my foot-
ing because I admitted that my familiar ways don't work, and I
don't yet know what to replace them with." Admitting a delusion
feels like an end—and it is. But it is also a beginning.

Learning something new often requires that we loosen our grip
on what is familiar and that we pass through a period of confusion before we can comprehend a new way. This program takes
us into personally uncharted territory, and the very first Step lays
out the hard truth. You may meet your powerlessness in attempts
to control the use of alcohol in another person's life. Or this Step
might apply to you when you exchange the word *alcohol* for
another word such as *drugs, money, sex, food, illness, divorce, emotions,
unemployment, death,* or *other people.* When you are willing and able
to identify your powerlessness, you have begun. Change always
brings discomfort, but the rewards in your life can be immense.

The First Step is like a political revolution within you. The forces
and powers that ran your life are thrown aside. The old order col-
lapses. Loyalty to what you thought was true, or right, or comfortable has to be questioned. You see more clearly than ever and
admit that old behaviors and old habits must be swept away. This
is the housecleaning that prepares you for your new beginning.
It is the moment of truth that cuts through your wishful thinking, illusions, and denials.

One woman tells about her undying belief that her boyfriend
would achieve his great potential if she continued to help him and
support him through the repeated crises he created by his drug
use. She was convinced that her lectures to him, her money to
pay his debts, her watchful eyes, and her affection would ultimately

prevail and free him from his drug dependency. Finally, true change began for her when she could see that all of her best efforts were leading to nothing.

With the First Step may come the crushing disappointment of realizing that you gave your heart and soul to a falsehood. It is the painful recognition that your best efforts to be good and play by the rules have a dark side of overcontrol and manipulation. Perhaps you developed self-righteous and smug attitudes that covered your low self-esteem and emotional pain. Perhaps you desperately believed that your good behavior could save your parent or spouse from harmful and self-defeating actions.

A friend we'll call Ron tells about the moment he realized he was powerless over his wife's problem with alcohol and that his life had become unmanageable. He was sent to Al-Anon by his therapist and went to six meetings in as many weeks. He thought, *This is a good place for all these people who have so many problems, but they are much worse off than I am.*

He knew that his wife, Nancy, was a troubled woman, and that she might be addicted to alcohol. She was the one who was obviously out of control and needed help. When they were together Ron took the job of keeping her satisfied and happy, monitoring how much wine was in the house and how much she drank each day. All during his waking hours Ron thought about helping Nancy. He tried to figure out her feelings and thoughts, and his main topic of discussion with his friends and co-workers was about her and what she said. In fact, her extreme and outrageous actions gave him wonderful material for many interesting stories. Sometimes his friends and co-workers were appalled, sometimes they would take Ron's side and tell him he was a saint for putting up with her, sometimes they were entertained or baffled, but eventually they all got tired of constantly talking about Nancy and Ron's relationship problems.

Ron was so absorbed in his wife's problems that he dropped the activities that refreshed and renewed him. He loved the movies, but it had been months since he was last inside a theater. He felt too exhausted, and he was always nervous about what Nancy would do while he was out of the house. Instead he spent his evenings in front of the TV and ate potato chips. He used to run three miles every day after work to stay in shape, but he didn't care to do that anymore. Most of his day was spent in negative feelings—worry, frustration, anger—and by evening he frequently had a headache and felt grumpy. Still, Ron didn't see that he needed any help for himself or that he ought to change. His only puzzle was about Nancy. The only answers he sought were about Nancy. "I'm fine, but she is a basket case! My problem is her," he said.

His new Al-Anon friends told him that he needed to look at his own actions, his powerlessness, not his wife's. They said it was probably true that Nancy needed help, but he could not fix or control her. They told him he needed help because his caretaking was part of the pattern that was maintaining a balance of chaos in his life, not fixing it. They said he was intensely distracted by Nancy and her problems, just as addicts are distracted by their drug of choice from taking good care of themselves.

At first, these were only words to Ron. He continued to go to Al-Anon meetings and to think about what they told him there, but it still didn't make much sense to him: "I'm supposed to admit my powerlessness over her and detach from her crazy actions. If I do that I might as well get a divorce because there won't be anything left of our relationship. We got married to be together, not to be detached!"

The more he thought about it, the more he began to like the idea of divorce. "It would be a way to get rid of my problem," he said. For two weeks he fretted over whether or not to get a divorce. In the morning he would decide divorce was the answer and by lunch he discarded the idea. Then by 2:00 P.M. he was weighing his choices all over again.

One sunny afternoon tragedy struck while Ron, a surveyor, stood behind his tripod on a country highway. The loud hiss of air brakes made him look up to see a sixteen-wheel truck speeding toward him. The driver had failed to see the "Construction Zone" warning signs until it was too late. Ron saw in a flash what was happening. As the driver tried to stop, the truck skidded out of control. The massive machine jackknifed and careened sideways toward him. Everything seemed to be happening in slow motion. Ron says, "I thought, *This is it! I am going to die!* Then for the next half-minute time seemed to just hang there. Everything in my life was suddenly simple. I knew clearly what I had to do. All the B.S.

dropped away. I knew in that instant that my scurrying around to take care of Nancy was a silly smoke screen. I knew that I loved her deeply and that my job was to deal with my own life, not hers. That's what I needed, not a divorce."

Ron woke up in the hospital with so many broken bones and injuries that he was there for five weeks. The instant his life became so simple was his First Step. It was the foundation for his emotional and spiritual recovery. It had begun at Al-Anon when he first heard the other members' comments, although he rejected them at the time. Now he was ready to go back to Al-Anon and admit, to himself most of all, that he was powerless over Nancy's actions and that his own life had become unmanageable.

He was no longer deluded by the thought that his only problems were Nancy's. He realized his attempts to control Nancy and her use of alcohol were his detour around confronting his own uncomfortable and painful issues. Now he felt like a rank beginner. This was a time when pain and hope were two sides of one coin. His pain was in emptying his cup and admitting that his most earnest efforts to help were not helpful, that his inner compass was set on misguided good intentions. He felt shocked to realize that he had a lot to learn, yet that was also his hope for the future.

A Radical Shift

The First Step is so radical a shift away from individual efforts to deal with problems that few will make the move until they have used up all other options. Rather than call it the First Step, we might call it a leap. People often say this Step feels like stepping off a cliff, not knowing where you will land. One Al-Anon member wisely observed that

> most of us cling to familiar answers as long as we can and only let go after we have tried every alternative— when we are finally desperate. We don't volunteer for this kind of leap; life problems push us off the ledge. If someone's system is working for them, they are not likely to put themselves through such turmoil for the sake of growth.

No one takes the First Step just once; you take it again and again. Gradually you incorporate its perspective on powerlessness into your personal philosophy of life. Who thinks of surrender as a good thing to do? Yet here is the paradox that the First Step teaches: Surrender is a choice. When you make the choice, you don't cave in like a passive victim to whatever comes along. Rather, you take the driver's seat by making a choice. You choose to be receptive and open to the benefits and strengths that other forces beyond your invention and control can provide. You can choose again to resist the inevitable to the very end, as you have been doing, or you can make a creative choice to surrender to it. The other side of surrender is peace.

Making the Move

The admission you make in the First Step is not like pleading guilty in court, admitting you did something wrong, or going through the motions to get it over with. Codependency and addiction survive on denial or distortion of the truth. The First Step is an awareness shift. First you admit the truth to yourself, then to trusted people around you. You let in the truth so that you can't continue blindly with habits that hurt you and those around you. Your consciousness is raised and you give up your license to do what you have done.

Grasping for control is the game of codependency. It keeps people stuck on a wretched treadmill, but again, the paradoxical First Step transforms your weakness into strength. When you accept your failure, you begin to win.

When you admit you can't control another's responses, you admit that a stone is rolling down a hill. Originally you had control when you set the stone in motion with a push at the top. You enjoyed it; you felt good, invigorated by your success and your power. But the stone has left your hands and now rolls on its own. You are no longer in control. What started it rolling is not what keeps it rolling. The stone keeps rolling by its momentum, and the new reality is that you are powerless.

Thinking about momentum shows you patterns. For example, a man remembers how during his childhood his father would come home drunk and abusive, but often settled down when distracted by his son's jokes. The boy's humor kept his brother and his mother from getting hit and pushed around. Ever since that time this man has used humor as a diversion from painful feelings. Whenever someone gets close to his feelings, he cracks a joke. What was helpful in the first instance has now become his automatic avoidance habit.

Another example of momentum is the woman whose husband used to praise her early in their marriage for making him feel worthwhile. She liked feeling helpful and successful and came to believe she could be responsible for his self-esteem. But over the years he actively destroyed all of his successes through a gambling addiction, and his self-esteem plummeted. She tried more vigorously than ever to prop him up with praise and support rather than stopping to say, *I admit that I am powerless over his addiction.*

Actions for Your First Step

How do you take this Step? How do you see yourself with a clearer lens? Perhaps you've had a moment of truth when your powerlessness came crashing into view, as it did for Ron. But many people don't have such a moment they can point to. Instead they have the ongoing feeling that something big is missing or wrong in their lives. In either case, you will repeatedly confront your powerlessness. You will need to do this Step many times and in many ways, each time deepening your awareness.

You can begin by making a list of all the ways you try to get control in your life and the lives of those you love. Either write down your list or say it out loud to a friend who has worked the First Step. Start with a focus on one specific substance or behavior, like alcohol or other drugs, food, sex, spending, gambling, smoking, or some other self-destructive action. Put on your list all the ways you watch, worry, preach, or try to control another's actions or use of the substance. Do you count his drinks? Do you watch what she takes from the refrigerator for snacks? Do you repeat yourself every day in an empty litany of persuasion? What about buying the substance for him? Do you buy it and then dole it out in measured quantities, closely monitoring how much it takes to get him drunk or high? Do you find it hard to say no to spending or to other behaviors that feel harmful to you? Do you reluctantly agree to her desires or her pleading and then try to manipulate the outcome? Do you feel caught in a no-win bind that leads you to feel guilty no matter what you do?

Another way to begin your First Step is to recall childhood times

43

when you were overwhelmed by someone's or something's power. This could be a situation in which you were abused. You could have felt deeply frightened, terrorized, or overstimulated. Maybe you were in an accident or some natural disaster that overwhelmed you. Maybe you first experienced powerlessness over a death or divorce. You can begin your First Step now by saying, "I was powerless over _____." Many children in that situation feel they did something wrong and were being punished for it, or think they caused the trouble. Sometimes adults blame children in those situations and tell them they have power that they don't actually have: "It's because you are so noisy that your father has to drink." Becoming a strong adult may mean abandoning your false childhood perceptions of power. These situations often overwhelm children and etch images into their memories that can be better healed by adult wisdom than by childhood attempts to cope.

Don't just remember these situations alone. The first word of the First Step is "We." In order to work the First Step, you must talk to a trusted friend, your Twelve Step group, or a therapist as you recall your experiences. A friend recounts these few helpful words she learned in treatment for family members: "You didn't cause it! You can't control it! You can't cure it!"

Another suggestion is to listen to your inner voice, your body's messages to you. It will tell you when you are feeling unsafe or afraid of losing control. For each person the signal is unique. Some call it butterflies in their stomach, some say they get a squeamish feeling or a tight feeling in their head. Your first impulse may be to control the situation, to manage the unmanageable, to take instant action and skip over your consciousness of these body signals. But they express a deep inner wisdom, and when you dismiss the signals you ignore your inner voice.

You can work your First Step by taking time to notice what your body tells you about your feelings. Then practice not doing anything about it right away—simply wait and notice how your body feels so you can make room for the wisdom to emerge into your consciousness. Tell yourself, *It's okay to feel antsy for a while without immediately fixing it.*

Step Two: Came to believe that a power greater than ourselves could restore us to sanity.

People often come to recovery when large parts of their lives are in stress and turmoil. Their marriage may be in disarray, they may face a court appearance, they may have painful relationships with parents, or they may have difficulties with child rearing. So the Second Step's promise of greater sanity feels welcome indeed. But people don't suddenly shed all their favorite rationalizations and denials simply by walking into their first meeting of Al-Anon. Many balk at the very suggestion that they need to be restored to sanity or that belief in a power greater than themselves is required.

Now in the Second Step you confront the core fact that the Twelve Step program is one of spiritual awakening and renewal. Those who already feel comfortable with the spiritual dimension in their life may have a leg up at the start. For others, spiritual language may seem alien, or a lot of hocus-pocus that holds out a false promise. Or perhaps for some religion was a negative influence in the past and they impulsively reject anything that smacks of it now.

For all starting points, the best advice we know is that *sound spirituality begins with your honesty,* not dogmatic teachings. Therefore, you should bring your true feelings with you, including your doubts and anger about spiritual ideas. As spirituality is understood here, your anger or your strong no! comes out of the place within you that says, *This is important. I can't take spiritual issues lightly.*

Equally important advice for all is to *leave your rigidity behind.* Whether you are committed to a clearly defined personal god or you are an atheist, you need not change your beliefs to grow in the Twelve Steps. But whatever your background, whatever your commitments, you will have to stay open to new learning in the spiritual realm.

The word *god,* as used here, has broader and more inclusive possibilities than many people learned in their past. From the beginning, this program was shaped by both agnostics and members of traditional religions. Out of their differences and conflicts about the wording of the Steps the founders learned to distinguish between religion and spirituality.

They said outright that *this is not a religious program.* Religion is a system of belief, ritual, and conduct held by a group of like-minded people; spirituality rests on personal experience, such as the feelings of awe and beauty inspired by nature, music, and art, or the deep emotions stirred by a relationship with another person or a higher power. Spirituality is a broader, more loosely defined concept than religion. It includes the affirming feelings of hope and joy that we find within us and the feelings of faith and determination that carry us forward through periods of dark struggle. It is our spiritual experience that moves us to feel that we are not merely separate, isolated individuals but part of a larger whole group, family, community, natural world, and universe. Spirituality leads us to ponder such ultimate mysteries as "What is the meaning of suffering?" It means noticing metaphors and messages in our experiences, such as the cycle of death and rebirth in the seasons and in many places in our own lives. Even the paper of the book in your hands is part of a cycle from earth and seed, sprout and tree, back to decay, earth, and new life. Spirituality means trusting your intuition, taking the concrete data of your life and staying open to its meaning, such as thinking, *Since I didn't get a job yet, perhaps I must rely on my higher power for something else that will ultimately be better for me.*

When you take this Step, there is little need to get into theology. A friend of ours tried diligently to define her concept of a higher power. She thought about traditional concepts of a personal god, she thought about nature and all the creative energies in the universe, until her sponsor suggested that she was misdirecting her attention for this Step. She said, "In the Second Step, you simply allow a ray of hope that your life can get better with help."

You may have lived so long with unresolved problems that you simply accept them as the way life is. You "normalized" what you could not change—or what you refused to change. You may feel deeply unworthy of a better life, or so hopeless that this Step seems impossible. You may feel you cannot hope, and may even be committed to staying hopeless. Hope may be such a big change that the first small increment is just to hope that you will find reason later to be hopeful.

Many people begin work on a specific Step by following the slogan "Act as if." For the Second Step, they go through the day not quite believing, but acting as if they did believe, that a greater power could restore them to sanity. This practice helps them open the door, helps them test the possibility that the principle could work in their lives.

You can make this Step very concrete by thinking of your Twelve Step group as the force outside yourself that brings hope to you. That might be your starting point: the higher power of love and the connections with people in your life.

If the tolerance and inclusiveness of the program seem wishy-washy at this point, let us underscore what is hard-core about this Step: *It asks you to place all hopelessness about yourself and all feelings of unworthiness on the shelf.* It also asks you to give up the idea that you have to do everything for yourself. If the First Step was a leap into the unknown, the Second Step is simply getting out of the way of healing forces.

Actions for Your Second Step

You may actually take one form of the Second Step before your First Step when you walk in the door of your first meeting—of Al-Anon or ACOA or CoDA. By going to the meeting you express some hope that this group will help you—and that is the Second Step. Of course, you still have a lot to learn. Your spiritual development may be just beginning. But that first move, without even thinking of it, may be the first time in a long while that you set aside hopelessness and doubt in favor of hope and confidence.

Did attending your first meeting frighten you? Did it take courage to go? Did it seem like more than just going to any ordinary meeting? You might understand the intensity of your feelings that day if you see that your inner stirring was a spiritual shift. You moved away from, or at least you weakened, the personal premise, *I am alone, I have to do it alone,* and moved toward a more spiritual premise: *Maybe someone else, maybe something else, can help me.* Every meeting you attend can be a concrete expression of your Second Step. Every time you call a fellow group member on the telephone or see him or her for coffee and feel the connection of your relationship, it is a form of the Second Step.

Another way you can do a Second Step is to find a place in nature that heals you and restores your serenity. It may be a walk in the park or on the beach, a stroll along a river bank, or a hike in the mountains. If you find yourself breathing easier, and the rest of your life concerns recede in your mind for a time, then this is the healing experience that comes from a power greater than ourselves. You go there not to make it happen, but to receive it. Perhaps you find it by playing with your dog or cat, or by gardening. In this program we understand that these moments are more than indulgences in our favorite activities or hobbies. They are essential because they restore us to our places in the whole, natural world. They provide spiritual renewal.

You can also do the Second Step by listening to an idea or suggestion that at first seems foreign or unacceptable. Rather than rejecting it immediately, hold onto it for a while as something that might help you. Don't get in the way of your higher power. Many times it's hard to tolerate the help you need because it doesn't fit what you already believe or want. In the past, your survival skills might have required you to live by your own wits. This is not to say that you need to become a compliant, passive, obedient robot. Retain your powers of discrimination.

Our friend Jim talks about leaving yourself open to possibilities:

> But if I understood everything and if I had all the answers I would not be human or need a community. The village is gone and my CoDA group is my peer group. So I try to do the Second Step by holding onto the suggestions and thoughts of others. I carry them with me and try them on, looking for the possibility that they may have some healing power that I could not give myself.

Step Three: Made a decision to turn our will and our lives over to the care of god as we understood god.

This Step is akin to many ancient spiritual and religious paths. For thousands of years, devout people around the earth have achieved some measure of personal growth through developing a trusting and receptive relationship to god as they understood god.

The Third Step gives you something to bump up against. If you don't feel resistant or defiant when you encounter it you probably have not really encountered it. It teaches you how much you want to get your own way. It shows you that you can become more fully human, that you can fulfill your potential by learning to rely on the care of god and by learning to do something very special with your own will and ego.

This is a relationship Step. It is a simple twenty-word statement. Yet one eager newcomer to the program missed its importance: "I'm going to learn the Twelve Steps as quickly as possible so I can get the basic idea and quit coming to meetings. I want to get on with my life and I don't see any point in dragging this out any longer than necessary." He thought going to his Twelve Step meeting was like taking a night class in adult education at his local high school—once you learn the concepts, you're on your own. When he heard the Step he quickly repeated it in his mind and thought: *Okay. I believe in God and living by the Ten Commandments. Let's go on to the next one.*

To follow this Step is like learning any skill, craft, or sport. A coach or teacher can tell you a simple message like "Keep your eye on the ball" or "Use only a light touch on the strings" or "Knead the dough until it develops a velvety texture," but understanding the words only points the way. You have not *learned* it until you have it in your body and in your experience. That takes disciplined practice. Once you learn the basics, you may continue to deepen and hone your skill for years. If you stop, you may get rusty.

This Step goes against conventional wisdom, which tells us that to become the best person we can be, we need to try harder and work at bringing forth our best behavior. Common wisdom touts the value of personal drive, determination, and a will to succeed as the keys to a good life. Those qualities are valuable, but they only reflect one side of personal strength.

The Third Step leads you into the kind of development that comes when you let your ego recede. It points to a very particular relationship with a higher power. This relationship, like any other, develops over time.

Wendell Berry expresses the meaning of the Third Step in his poem at the top of page 50.

49

THE PEACE OF WILD THINGS

When despair for the world grows in me
and I wake in the night at the least sound
in fear of what my life and my children's lives may be,
I go and lie down where the wood drake
rests in his beauty on the water, and the great heron feeds.
I come into the peace of wild things
who do not tax their lives with forethought
of grief. I come into the presence of still water.
And I feel above me the day-blind stars
waiting with their light. For a time
I rest in the grace of the world, and am free.

—Wendell Berry

Turning your will and your life over to the care of god does not mean you stop being responsible for your life or that there is no longer any room for what you want. This Step emphasizes the *care* of god. You allow yourself to be directed by the loving and benevolent will of god. That will manifests itself to you in many ways.

Family therapist David Berenson says, "As one opens to a spiritual reality, there is a dramatic increase in the number of . . . meaningful coincidences that start occurring."[5] In this Step, that means you see spiritual meaning deeper than the mere law of averages when you happen to run into a friend just at the moment you need some help. When you feel the *connection* in the relationship you know a telephone call from a friend is not just a routine call to convey a message, but a spiritual experience.

For example, John D. was in Adult Children of Alcoholics. He was planning to go out for his routine walk one day but the rain forced him to stay indoors. So with time on his hands he spontaneously picked up a book that had lain around for over a year. In the warm, dry coziness of his favorite chair he read a chapter that spoke so personally to him that it changed the way he understood his whole childhood. The coincidence of the rain that led to his reading the book had a personal spiritual meaning for him. His Third Step outlook awakened him to the care of god that created this moment. The Third Step made him receptive to new information.

You have experienced the spiritual principle of the Third Step when you have tried to recall a name that would not come to mind. The harder you try to remember, the more the name seems to slip out of reach. But after you stop trying and go on to other things, perhaps on your way home or in a quiet moment, the name suddenly pops into your mind, as if out of nowhere. Similar experiences happen for many people when they struggle with a problem all day and go to bed that night with it unsolved. The next morning, getting ready for the day, seemingly without even thinking about it, the answer becomes clear.

Actions for Your Third Step

One suggestion for practicing the Third Step can be used whenever you are worried about something or you have a decision to make: *Allow time and space for your higher power to lead you.* Take your time; don't rush toward a solution. Sleep on it. Pray about it by talking to your higher power just as you would to a wise and loving sage. Talk to friends to see what they think. Notice how your body feels as you think about various alternatives.

One woman was always frustrated in traffic and angry when other drivers got in her way. She decided she would learn the Third Step through her driving. Instead of honking her horn, swearing and gesturing at other drivers, she thought to herself, *I'm turning over my anger and my impatience to the care of god. That doesn't mean god will give me what I want. It means god can take care of my anger and impatience and I can get out of the way.* She found that she began arriving at her destinations feeling peaceful and, ironically, more in charge of herself.

The Third Step can work for you when you are bothered by guilt or remorse about past mistakes that you can do nothing to repair, or when you become obsessed with things that you feel powerless to control. You can then fall back into the care of god and consciously say, *I'm turning it over to god because there's nothing I can do about it. I can't fix it and I can't control my mind, so I will just let god handle it.* You will find that you probably can do that for a short while until suddenly you have taken it on again and start churning it in your mind. Then you have to turn it over again.

One man who was deeply worried about his wife's cancer said,

51

"I know I can only turn it over to god, and whenever I do I settle down and can work better at what I can control. But it seems like I have to do that a hundred times a day because I keep forgetting myself and picking it up again."

Dr. Joseph Sittler, a noted theologian, advised that we can grow spiritually when we explore "the lurking meaning behind the obvious world."[6] How can you learn to uncover those subtle truths that lay quietly behind your ordinary daily experiences? Many approaches can help. You can attend retreats; read Scriptures, novels, poetry, and other literature; appreciate beauty; participate in massage and body work; do daily meditation; visit sacred places; get close to nature; work for peace and justice; volunteer to help at a place that feeds the hungry or cares for the ill; listen to music; or get a spiritual director, a person who has been trained in guiding people in their spiritual growth.

Some people in the program have used other schematic systems for gaining increased sense of self and spirituality. They include: the Enneagram, an ancient system from the Sufis of Persia, now gaining recognition among some traditional religious leaders in the West, which describes the habits of heart and mind of nine personality types and their interrelationships;[7] Chakras, a system of energy centers located at points in the body, studied for centuries in India;[8] and the Myers-Briggs Type Indicator, a tool for discovering personality types used in modern psychology.[9]

Native Americans use the Sweat Lodge and Vision Quest in traditional spiritual practices, and many non-Native Americans have also found them meaningful.[10] The *I Ching or Book of Changes* was written in China thousands of years ago as a spiritual mentor to those seeking wisdom in how to respond to the problems in their lives.[11] Although ancient, it is surprisingly congruent with the Twelve Steps. Taking a modern translation, some people find guidance for their choices, even in complicated contemporary life. As you care for your spiritual self, you feel cared for.

The wisdom of Zen tells us that spiritual growth is not a thing we can achieve and hold; rather, it is a dynamic process that happens by continuous return to an ideal. The Third Step teaches us to turn things over to the care of god, not in one ultimate move, but completely—over and over again. "Progress—not perfection" is the traditional slogan for growth in the program.

My purpose is to know my true self and know serenity.

CHAPTER FOUR

Trust shows the way.
—Hildegarde of Bingen

Looking in the Mirror With an Honest and Loving Friend: Seeing Who You Really Are

Step Four: Made a searching and fearless moral inventory of ourselves.

Step Five: Admitted to god, to ourselves, and to another human being the exact nature of our wrongs.

*B*eginning a recovery program for codependency is *a process for changing your life.* By doing the first three Steps, you have become willing to hope that your life may be changed. You have let some trust come into your life. By taking the first three Steps you have acknowledged that you have been leading a life that is false in some respects, that you have been more concerned for others—and other people's opinions of you—than for your own well-being. You have been living through others rather than living through your own experiences.

What can you do to learn how to have a healthy concern for your own welfare? At this stage, you may have heard the phrase *Take care of yourself,* yet you may not have the foggiest notion of what that means. So we're not going to say that here! What we will say is that working the Steps is a process that will let you discover how to take care of yourself.

One of the reasons you may not know how to take care of yourself is that you haven't seen who you really are. Your development as a separate individual has been delayed. So the

55

first thing you have to do is try to see yourself and your situation objectively.

To see yourself objectively, it may help to think of codependency as something like cancer, because the visual picture can give you a sense of the "otherness" of cancer. Your codependency is not *you*. Codependency-as-cancer means that a destructive process has invaded the boundary between you and the rest of the world. You have been taken over by the needs and demands of others, or the culture at large, which demands sacrifice and conformity, or some kind of "less-than" picture of selfhood. Codependency is *not* your natural, healthy self, which is always with you, even though codependency has grabbed you by the throat.

When you can imagine codependency like cancer, you can imagine it as being separate from you, and you can imagine it leaving your body and your life. You can also imagine the seriousness of its impact on you and the danger it presents to you. It is very important to see how it is hurting you and others.

Steps Four and Five are the tools for *seeing* the extent of codependency in your life, for assessing the harm it has done, and for getting a realistic sense of what is actually happening. You can think of Steps Four and Five as an X ray of the tumor that grew without your even noticing. With this X ray, you can begin figuring out what you want to change and how you want to be changed: Surgery? Chemotherapy? A laying on of hands? Natural remission?

Step Four: Made a searching and fearless moral inventory of ourselves.

This Step brings to mind many associations: *Search* suggests a journey, an adventure, a discovery of forgotten treasure. *Inventory* suggests taking stock of the warehouse, counting up assets as well as deficiencies. *Moral* suggests values and the evaluation of values. Because it doesn't say whose morals, you are given the freedom in this program to discover your own values. Values become clear when you work the Steps, tell your story, go to meetings, and meditate about god's will for your life. In this way, the program gives you a practical sequence of actions for discovering the purpose of your life, and the freedom to choose.

This Step is perhaps the one most feared by people because it sounds overwhelmingly guilt-ridden, shaming. It is frightening to contemplate mistakes. But we notice the word *fearless*. Why is this a fearless search? Because the first three Steps give assurance that recovery is a loving process. The word *fearless* says that you can look directly into the mirror and not be afraid. A higher power may have the shape of a loving and honest friend who sees you as you are and accepts both your strengths and weaknesses.

So when you set out to do Step Four, it is important to do it only when you are able to have an honest and loving attitude toward yourself. Step Four should not be done as an opportunity to indulge in shame and dwell on all the awful sins you have committed. Why not? Shame begets shame. If you did your Step Four and didn't look at your strengths, you might get stuck in shame rather than acknowledging less-than-perfect behaviors and moving on.

So how do you begin Step Four?

Pretend you are standing in front of a full-length mirror and ask yourself some questions about yourself and your life. Look at the whole picture.

What do you see that you like? Is there still the hint of a smile somewhere on your face? Now look deeper:

- What do I value in myself?
- What area of my life needs integration?
- Which of my behaviors would I like to see a change in?
- Have I been acting like a crazy person, and in what situations?
- What behaviors are hurting me?
- What are my values and how have I violated them?
- How would I be if I were experiencing healing?
- What do I want to work on this year?
- How is my physical health?
- How is codependency running wild in my life?
- What is it that I'm not doing that I would like to be doing but think I can't do because I'm so preoccupied (tired, tense, exhausted, busy) with another person's addiction?
- What secrets am I keeping?
- What do I feel guilty about?

These general questions can give you a holistic look at yourself and your situation. As you look at your situation, you can break it into parts to write an assessment of the extent of the codependency. For example, you might write out some short answers to these questions and then decide that you want to take a look at three primary concerns: (1) control issues; (2) fear, worry, and insecurity (which you may see as a lack of trust in your higher power); and (3) physical health.

You can sit down and do free writing about each issue. Let your thoughts ramble but keep the focus on the behavior and how it manifests itself in your life. For example, one writer wrote the following passage about her compulsive eating:

> Before I sit down to work, I want something to eat. I walk up to the convenience store for a bag of Pepperidge Farm cookies. Back home, I put the bag on the sideboard and go upstairs to work. I clear off my work space, find paper, dig up the book I am supposed to review, glance through at the notes I made when I read it the first time. All I can think about is the cookies on the sideboard. Obviously this review is going to take all day. It's time for a break.
>
> I go downstairs and put water on for tea, measure loose Darjeeling into a tea ball, and choose a mug. I open the cookies. Deep down I know that I am going to eat all of the cookies before I go back to work, but first I am going to try not to. When the water boils, I make my tea, and because no one else is home, I take my tray into the living room.
>
> They are my very favorite cookies, and I eat them slowly, savoring the taste. I pour my tea. My feet are walking to the kitchen for two more cookies, then two more; if my housemates find half a bag of cookies in the kitchen, they will know that I ate the other half, so I might as well finish them off. I eat the rest one after the other, hardly noticing how they taste, feeling only the way they clog my throat and finally come to rest like a lump in my belly. I am disgusted with myself. I feel sick.
>
> —Susanna J. Sturgis

Because the writer lets herself stay with the details of the behavior, she is able to *see* the extent of her intense relationship with Pepperidge Farm. In writing out the extent of this obsession, you somehow clear the path for the obsession to be released. Only when you see something clearly are you able to let go of it.

By doing free writing, you gain understanding of your present behaviors and see the impact that these behaviors have on your life. Step Four lets you know what you know. You let the right hand see what the left is doing.

Some people don't want to do this much writing and may choose to do this Step by following a traditional Step Four guide with a printed list of assets and liabilities. But it is worth trying some free writing, whichever kind of Step Four you do. If you are using a traditional list, take a look at these qualities and write down the ones that are hurting you. For example, if you have a problem with perfectionism, give a few examples of how this has caused a problem in your life. What have you done out of perfectionism that you feel guilty about? If you feel guilty, let the guilt guide you into making the list of things you've done that you wish you hadn't.

A third way to work is to do a focused Step Four. Select *one area* of your life and look at its history. One man did an inventory of shame and how it affected his whole life. Another woman did an inventory of her life as a mother in order to gain perspective on her current situation with her adolescent daughter, who was acting out. The mother was concerned about boundaries, her own control issues, and whether or not she was enabling her daughter's self-destructive behavior.

Because she limited her focus to her life as a mother, she was free to bring in a flood of memories that might have seemed irrelevant if she'd been trying to cover everything. She remembered her daughter's tantrums when she was three and left at day care. The child would lie on the sidewalk and kick her sturdy oxfords. The mother remembered the day her daughter's cat died and how she howled all day, refusing to be consoled. Her personality had always tended toward melodrama. These memories helped the mother see that the adolescent acting out was similar to her behavior as a toddler and, as such, was within her normal behavior range. The mother could see her own behavior as a mother more objectively in light of the child's development.

A focused Step Four gives perspective to life situations. It gives the long view, the historical context, the life development. It gives the depth you need to look at your present situation. An intense engagement with one issue eventually shifts your perspective on everything else in your life.

Actions for Your Fourth Step

Pick the method that feels most suitable for you to work on. Before you start writing, set a reasonable deadline for completion. Having a deadline will prevent you from dragging on and on and never finishing. Some people make their Fifth Step appointment when they begin to work on Step Four so that they will have closure on the activity and the anxiety.

Additional Step Four Issues

What are typical areas people look at in an inventory? Most people who identify themselves as having trouble with codependency are also struggling with issues of control. Many people who try to control were victimized as children, and the loss of control that they experienced then—the helplessness—was so terrifying that they only feel safe when they feel in control. Paradoxically, people who were victimized in the past often get into situations in which they are being victimized and controlled again. This does not happen because the people are masochists. It probably happens because victimization probably destroyed their natural warning system. Part of recovery is learning what a warning system is and then developing one.

At many meetings, it is usual to hear someone say something like the following:

> My purpose in this program is to see to it that I'm in situations where I'm not being abused or abusing myself.

You may read this and say, "That's it? That's all this guy wants? He doesn't want happiness, fulfillment, etc.?" Of course a person may want more, but safety is a primary need. A man who feels safe in the world has learned a complex set of behaviors: what abuse is, the connection between outer environment and inner feelings, how to establish boundaries and set limits, how to change boundaries, and how to leave a situation that is unhealthy. Working the Steps is one way to learn these means of self-care. Working the Steps is the process of learning what self-care is.

The following are some other typical issues that codependency usually drags into the house:

- panic
- anxiety
- fear/catastrophizing
- obsessive thoughts
- preoccupation with feelings of abandonment
- perfectionism
- rage and hysterical outbursts (both men and women)
- saying things indirectly (sarcasm)
- quiet grudges and resentment (stifled anger)
- shame (feeling like nothing, feeling worthless)
- neglecting physical health (exercise, good food, personal appearance)
- overworking
- isolating
- numbing out—not knowing what your feelings are
- sexual problems
- making too many commitments and then feeling crazy because you can't get everything done
- chemical dependency, eating disorders, and other compulsive behaviors
- being self-righteous and judgmental

This list is not a checklist of "characteristics" of codependent actions. As authors, we do not believe in the idea of a checklist of codependency, that is, a list that can determine that people are codependent if they check off 80 percent of the items. We think each person gets to decide which behaviors are codependent. Each item on this list may indicate codependent behavior, but some of the characteristics on this list also apply to many people who don't think of themselves as codependent. Our viewpoint is that people have to decide for themselves which traits are indicative of codependency and which are indicative of something else, such as an eating disorder. We believe that *codependent* is a label that people should use only in terms of their own behaviors; nobody else gets to label particular behaviors of other people as codependent. *Behaviors* are codependent, and people may or may not exhibit codependenency through the behaviors on this list.

You are the person who knows—or will learn to know—which behaviors are dangerous and destructive to you. The knowledge comes from within you.

And as you do your inventory, you don't have to think about making these behaviors go away; just admit, as you did in Step One, that you wish to heck you didn't have a stomachache every morning.

A last cautionary note—as you do your inventory there are two extremes to watch out for: first, that you don't spend an endless amount of time going into detail on each item so that you start feeling hopeless and never finish the Step; and second, the opposite extreme—that you'll work too much on the surface and dismiss some behaviors too lightly.

Remember the Friend at Your Side

After you've looked at some of the behaviors you feel guilty about, think of the person at your side who is your friend in spite of your secrets and imperfections. This friend sees more than flaws. What does he or she see? Make a list or write a short description of your good qualities, qualities that a good friend appreciates. Loyalty? Sure, maybe you've gone overboard on your loyalty and stayed with abusive people too many years, but loyalty is a gift that a healthy friend treasures. Maybe you love to stand on the bridge over the river and look at the light on the water each morning. A good friend appreciates and admires your love of the aesthetic.

Life Changes, Inventories Change

After you have done the Steps once and come around again to Step Four, you may look at totally different behaviors. Life gives you new situations to deal with every year, and different aspects of your being are called forth.

For example, the man we quoted earlier who strives to live a life free of abuse might say in a few years:

> My purpose is to be myself, to know serenity, to re-
> lax every day, to honor my work, to let god be at work
> in my life.

The Steps change as life changes. The reason the Steps change is that they are a process, a structure for people to move through, not a list of rules.

Step Five: Admitted to god, to ourselves, and to another human being the exact nature of our wrongs.

Our chapter title suggests that these two Steps are like look- ing in a mirror with a friend. Your higher power sees who you are and accepts both your strengths and weaknesses. Step Four is the act of looking in the mirror honestly, and Step Five is the act of letting a friend see the face in the mirror also.

Steps Four and Five are two halves of a whole; each comple- ments the other. As you work on Step Four, you are preparing to do Step Five. Step Four is reflection; Step Five is action, let- ting another person in. As with so many of the Steps, there is a give-and-take here between action and reflection. This give-and- take gives the Steps their motion, their forward momentum. As you do Step Five, you are releasing the tension that built up as you prepared your inventory and contemplated revealing it to another person.

What exactly is this tension? Tension can be described as a phys- ical response to feelings of fear, shame, dread, or guilt. Before contemplating the Step, it is good to remember that just as you did the inventory with a loving attitude, so too will you carry out Step Five with a love for yourself and your life.

Step Five directs people to admit the wrongs discovered in the Step Four inventory to another person. The focus of this Step is always on talking out loud to another person. The act of talk- ing makes the written inventory more real than if it stayed on paper. Somehow the Step makes talking to another person the link between god, self, and community.

People in the program carry out the action of this Step in several ways. Many seek out a minister or counselor who is known as someone who "hears" Fifth Steps. Often this activity will be the only contact between the two parties. This anonymity gives the Step a special ritual feeling.

Other people may feel comfortable talking with a spiritual counselor, such as a pastor, rabbi, or other religious leader who is very much a part of their life.

Many people new to the program want to know what happens during a Fifth Step. Because this is confidential, it would be hard for anyone to generalize. But we've talked with people about how they've done it. Most people bring their written inventory from Step Four to the meeting. Some read their notes. Others simply talk about what they've discovered by doing an inventory. This talking releases their guilt and shame over actions that have caused harm to themselves and others. There is a release from the past.

The person who is hearing the Fifth Step is a witness, and the presence of this person is what helps the past to be released. The person may not say much. During the session, many feelings may be experienced: grief, sorrow, remorse, anger, fear, as well as joy over the good things that have come to pass.

If you're preparing to do a Fifth Step, you may have a lot of fear. The person who is listening is not going to gloss over things that you've done that were wrong—fear is understandable. The act of talking means that you are going to be held accountable for what you've done. You may have done things you regard as unethical, even illegal. It is normal to be scared of admitting mistakes, wrongs, shortcomings. Fear is a normal part of this process.

But when you feel overwhelmed by fear, remember again the honest and loving friend in the chapter title. The person hearing your Fifth Step has made a commitment to be honest and loving. Honesty means not glossing over mistakes, and loving means seeing your good qualities and finding forgiveness. Many people report that after a Fifth Step, they could see good qualities about themselves that they hadn't recognized before. They also say that taking the Step helped them figure out where they were being too hard on themselves.

A loving friend helps you avoid the pitfall of perfectionism and forgive yourself for the mistakes you've made.

In closing, it's useful to note that it is a mistake to put off doing your Fifth Step. Procrastination is itself a demon. Try to do a Fifth Step as soon as you're done with your inventory. It will bring you a tremendous sense of relief. And you don't have to do it perfectly, because you don't do the Steps only once. If there's something you missed, you'll get it the next time around.

When you leave your Fifth Step meeting, you will have a new awareness of who you are.

Actions for Your Fifth Step

Find out the names of some people who hear Fifth Steps and choose one. Set up an appointment. If you're afraid, talk to someone else in the program about your fear.

I am poised on the edge of a new reality.

CHAPTER FIVE

Basic Forgiveness Affirmations
1. I forgive myself for hurting others.
2. I forgive others for hurting me.
3. I forgive myself for letting others hurt me.
— Phil Laut

A New Picture of Reality: Letting Change Happen

Step Six: *Were entirely ready to have god remove all these defects of character.*

Step Seven: *Humbly asked god to remove our shortcomings.*

When you have completed Steps Four and Five, you have given yourself an honest, realistic, loving self-portrait. It's an up-to-date report on where you are now. You see who you are, who you have become. You see aspects of yourself that seem false and that you would like to change. So what's next?

Are you supposed to get right to work and eliminate perfectionism and other destructive habits from all areas of your life? No, that probably wouldn't work.

What's next is being able to imagine a new picture of reality: Picture yourself as someone who is being transformed, changing and changed. What does this picture look like? Obviously, we're not talking simple changes in appearance, like make-overs on a TV show, with before-and-after shots. But imagining yourself in a before-and-after picture could help you imagine change. For example, if you know that worry is a character defect of yours, you might imagine yourself when you are worried, anxious, and frantic—how you look, act, and sound, how your body feels. Then imagine yourself relaxed. What would change about your outer and inner picture if this change took place?

When you do Steps Six and Seven, you become willing to move into that new picture of yourself.

Step Six: Were entirely ready to have god remove all these defects of character.

The primary message of this Step is simply that god is the one who is in charge of change. The individual person, the one with the ego, is not the one who makes these defects go away. Conventional wisdom says that if you want to change badly enough, you will do so with the force of will. In the experience of people in this program, however, the human ego and willpower are not effective in changing character.

Implicit in this Step is a tremendous sense of relief. It's a pause, a break, a time for refreshment.

After all the intensity and fear of doing Steps Four and Five, Step Six offers the promise that god is present in human imperfection. Step Six offers hope after the pain of recognizing your failings.

This Step holds the promise, like Step Two, that you don't have to do it alone.

So before you do anything else, just "be." Be present to your own character. Be with it, without fighting it. Be in your life, as it is. You will notice that the first words of this Step are *Were entirely ready*. The idea of this phrase is *being*, not doing. *Being ready* is a spiritual condition. *Being ready* is learning how to sit still with yourself, as you are. *Being ready* is a vulnerability, an opening, even though you have no knowledge of what will happen next.

What does it mean to be ready? The word *ready* suggests a willingness, an openness. Ready also suggests a certain sense of completion with the past, as when someone says, "I'm ready to start an aerobics program." Past exercise classes and any halfhearted attempts are forgotten.

But being ready doesn't mean that you have to do anything. You can be ready and waiting for a long time before anything happens. There is a mystery to how change happens, when it happens, and why.

A common saying in Twelve Step meetings is, "Everyone has their own timetable." Change can happen in some areas quickly and be as slow as molasses in others. God also has a sense of time, and when doing this Step, we remember that it is god who is determining the timetable.

But there are some things a person can do to become ready. Even though this Step says, "We were ready," people confess that they're not. If you're not ready, what can you do?

You can take some time alone, find a place where you feel relaxed, and sit back and contemplate that new picture of yourself. Let yourself *see* a change: How would you look if you were free of worry merely an hour a day? Rehearse a few scenes; that is, imagine yourself in the world doing your daily routine in a relaxed fashion. What's different?

Another way of becoming ready is to examine one character defect, such as worry, and ask yourself some questions about it: *What would happen to me if I didn't worry about money? What feelings would I have?* Some people might answer this question by saying loss of control, others say everything would fall apart and they'd feel guilty. Still others know they feel a vague sense of worry when they're not worrying. . . .

Now you might ask, *What is worry doing for me? What am I getting out of worrying?* Most people who worry think that they're putting energy into a situation and "getting it under control," and they feel more secure.

Lastly, ask yourself, *If worry were removed from my life, would I feel empty? Would I recognize myself?* Relaxing and letting yourself "be" with a character defect is one way to become ready. Remember that you are only being with it, you are not supposed to get into the control mode and try to make it go away. The change will happen according to another timetable.

Some people in the program choose more active methods of becoming ready, such as going into therapy to work on a particular defect or taking a great deal of time for rest and meditation on the defect. If you are really stuck on your money issues, you might consult with a variety of people—a therapist, a financial counselor, a spiritual director—for insights, for some advice to jar you loose, for clarity. This active work can be a valid way to reach the point of being ready.

Even so, you need to continue to acknowledge that change happens in mysterious ways. It's not up to you to make your defect go away.

Actions for Your Sixth Step

Set aside time this week to be with one of your character defects. Let yourself feel what it would be like for you if it went away. Ask yourself questions about it. Ask yourself if you need to talk with another person about it. Meditate on the thoughts in this chapter. Ask for acceptance of yourself as you are.

Step Seven: Humbly asked god to remove our shortcomings.

After a person feels ready to have shortcomings removed, it is time to ask for this to happen. It's almost as though Step Six is a meditation and Step Seven is a prayer.

Your prayer may be as simple as *Okay, I'm ready to give it up. I'm not holding on to worry anymore. Please lift it from my life.* Or your prayer may be more urgent if you feel desperate: *God, you said you'd lift this from me. I've been doing my best and I can't handle it anymore. So if you mean it, you have to take it from here.* Other feelings may be associated with prayer, even anger and annoyance, as in the prayer of someone who has felt a hint of reassurance but has trouble believing it and says, "Okay, okay I hear you." There are many ways to ask for something; the emphasis is on asking, not making it happen.

You'll notice that the Step doesn't say *when* or *if* these shortcomings will be removed. People who have been in the program a long time attest to the fact that change does happen, but usually not in the way that was expected. There are several ways people describe changes that are a result of this Step.

Some Shortcomings Disappear Slowly

Sometimes a person may ask for a shortcoming to be released, and it eventually seems to dissolve or dissipate after much time, thought, and prayer. For example, most people in the program want to change their reactive style of living. They want to give up what's called crisis living. They want to give up being *intensity junkies.* They want to make decisions and even live out the advice of "Let the chips fall where they may." They like the consolation of clichés because they reveal some timeless truth about the world.

Gradually, the highs and lows even out and people learn to take life in stride, more peaceably. This change is slow, subtle, and one that most people are extremely grateful to experience. The experience involves changes in thinking patterns, body chemistry, and a certain detachment from one's own emotions.

When people in the program are able to accept the idea of gradual change rather than a quick fix, it is partly because they've given up striving for perfection. The process of the Steps helps people accept their imperfections. People learn to value the seasons, their own unconscious timetable, the natural course of events. Many share the outlook of Matthew Fox:

> When you build your basic understanding of the universe on nature's cycles . . . rather than on a mythical past state of perfection . . . you learn to reverence change and process.[1]

Sometimes More Is Given than Requested

Asking for help carries its own power. You are making progress in your life when you can ask for anything. Anything! Asking to change something in your own character demands faith and humility and hope. The surprise for people in the program is that often the change is better than expected. For example, one woman who struggled with codependency and depression decided to pray that after waking up in the morning, she would experience dread for only the first two hours of her waking day. She made this prayer for several months. Then, as often happens, she forgot about the prayer and drifted on to other concerns. One day she woke up, feeling rather optimistic after only one cup of coffee. She looked around the room in surprise: *What has happened to my demon dread?* She realized she hadn't experienced dread for quite some time, and was more completely free of it than she'd ever imagined possible. She smiled to herself as she realized she could now truly live out the saying, "Don't trouble trouble 'til trouble troubles you."

A man in Al-Anon was obsessed with running a marathon. He realized that his obsession was taking him away from his work life, his family, and his friends. He asked that the obsessive quality of his running be taken away from him. He wanted to be able to enjoy running—to train hard, run one marathon a year, then relax and enjoy other parts of his life the rest of the time. You might imagine that he was surprised when his obsession totally disappeared—it didn't just go into remission, it vanished. He not only quit obsessing about running, he was incapable of doing it at all anymore. It was all or nothing—maybe because, like many people in the program, he was an all-or-nothing kind of guy. Moderation is not an easy quality to have. Although a person may want moderation, it may only appear in *some* areas of life.

When a character defect disappears totally, a person may be thrown into a whirlpool of conflicting feelings: loss, sorrow, joy, relief, amazement, awe at the mystery of the human condition. If this happens to you, you may say with the runner, who lost something that was good as well as bad, *Well, my higher power sees fit for that not to be in my life anymore. It's a mystery to me why that is.*

Working the Program Releases Unacknowledged Shortcomings

One of the miracles of the program is that peoples' characters change over time, sometimes without their conscious knowledge and control. Leading a life that is on an even keel leads to positive changes that could not have been predicted.

One woman who had worked the program for many years experienced one of these benefits when she realized that she was not envious of her friend when her friend enjoyed great financial success. "You know," she said, "I'm gratified to be able to feel unabated joy at my friend's success. This is such a gift. A few years ago I was envious. This change has come about from concentrating on other parts of my work, especially through Step Three. I have never identified envy as a shortcoming, but I have been practicing turning everything over."

Another person had experienced fear of flying but had never identified it as a shortcoming. It seemed too trivial to be a shortcoming, yet it caused him a lot of agonizing. He anticipated trips with great apprehension. After seven years in the program, he was scheduled to fly again. He got on the plane, read a book, and enjoyed take-off. *What's happening to me?* he thought. *I'm not the same person.* Perhaps his work in the program on letting go and trusting helped him to enjoy the change.

Some Shortcomings Stick Around

You'd be in shock if god took away all your shortcomings at once. You'd have to ascend to the heavens immediately. You wouldn't recognize yourself.

But many people are frustrated when they do their work and their shortcomings don't budge. Many people talk about really wanting to let go of something and being unable to. It is a mystery why hard work does not pay off in some cases! One woman wanted to be more lighthearted and fun-loving, but she kept getting stuck in her compulsive work habits. She identified the problem: "My parents didn't raise me to be a man or a woman, they raised me to be a workhorse."

The program teaches that when a shortcoming is not removed, there is a reason it is not removed. God has a timetable. A person may continue to struggle, pray, and let go.

There is tension between the words *struggle* and *let go*. This tension is part of the natural order of life, opposites that are somehow part of each other. Stop for a minute and think of the many life situations in which struggling and letting go seem to go hand in hand.

- Swimming—having strong strokes and being carried by the water at the same time.
- Tending a garden—and yet knowing that the summer storms and sun that affect its growth are out of your control.
- Toilet training a child—knowing that the struggle will continue until you let go.

All valiant changes have elements of both struggle and letting go. An old slogan captures this ambiguity: "Joy in the struggle!"

During the struggling stage of any change, you need to keep in mind the fact that change is slow, that some shortcomings may never change, and that even a small amount of change may work wonders. Even a small change can have enormous positive consequences and reverberations in your life, and that is something worth working for. The woman whose dread disappeared for no reason found that she had more energy, more optimism, and more time for herself and her family. It affected her whole life.

Let's say you are struggling with perfectionism. Most people who struggle with codependency are really hooked on

73

perfectionism—they take on too much work, want everything to turn out just right, and berate themselves when things go wrong. What's more, some people are so successful in controlling themselves and their situation *perfectly* that they feel they have achieved a status in life that others should aspire to. Their very accomplishments may make it more difficult to let go of their codependent behaviors. Letting go of a piece of this perfectionism can spread and have a ripple effect on the rest of your life. If you let yourself cancel a few meetings that you "should" attend, you may discover that you are also more relaxed about your expectations for your children. You may discover that your conversations with your friends are more fun. But even struggling to let go of one small piece can seem very difficult. The writer Lee Orcutt Rohwer has described her struggle to let go of perfectionism in the poem "An Old Habit."

AN OLD HABIT

I am gathering pinecones for the children,
I am careful to select only the perfect ones.

For some reason I think of Martin, whose brain
abscess happened in a 1944 town too small and too

cautious to use penicillin. I think of the time
he spilled Coke all over his lap. Skinny, curled

into himself, head too big for his body, slobber
strung from his slightly open mouth. He had

responded to the spill in his slow, measured manner,
"Oh - well - most - of - it - just - runs - down -

my - chin - anyway!" Grinning hugely at his own
humor while swiping at his lap with his good arm,

he made matters worse,
causing us to laugh harder.

I stop discarding broken, limp pinecones;
I will explain to the children that

God loves each and every one of us,
no matter how we look.

But my mind wanders and I catch myself
again selecting only perfect pinecones.

I make a renewed effort not to. I repeat this
process four times before the sack is full.
                                —Lee Orcutt Rohwer

The mystery of why some things change and not others is
enough to give you a sense of humility.

In fact, you'll note that the word *Humbly* is the first word of
this Step. What does *humbly* mean to you? Humility? *Humbly*
comes from the word *humus,* meaning earth, the soil that feeds
us. The word reminds us that we are creatures of the earth. We
are physical beings, with all the quirks, aches and pains, worries,
and anxieties that come with having a physical body in the
material world. We are not disembodied minds floating in the
clouds. We are not angels, intellects, hearts. By living out our lives,
we will unavoidably take some actions and make some decisions
that cause harm to other people. This cannot be avoided. We are
by nature imperfect.

As you think of the background to this word, you can see that
Humbly in the context of this Step reminds you that you are not
expected to be perfect. The old phrase "humble yourself" means
to *acknowledge your humanity.* You are a physical being, and your
higher power is guiding you. Some of your shortcomings will
be removed, others will stay, new ones will probably arise. What
you no longer need will be removed.

The idea that your higher power is in charge of change is a gift
of freedom.

Actions for Your Seventh Step

To bring a sense of closure to your work on this Step, you might imagine a picture or scene that represents freedom to you.

Take some time to focus on one shortcoming you'd like to go away. What can you do that would symbolize your willingness to let go of it? Write a prayer? Pray every morning? Talk to a friend about your desire for it to change? Talk with your higher power every day on the bus to work?

Honesty refreshes me and deepens my relationships.

CHAPTER SIX

*Truthfulness, honor, is not something which springs
ablaze of itself; it has to be created between people.*

—Adrienne Rich

Saying Good-bye to Shadows: Making Amends for the Past So You Can Move On

*Step Eight: Made a list of all persons we had harmed, and became
willing to make amends to them all.*

*Step Nine: Made direct amends to such people wherever possible, ex-
cept when to do so would injure them or others.*

A program of spiritual growth sounds intangible, mystical, and hard to get your hands onto. But in many ways, the spirituality of the Twelve Steps has a foundation of stone and mortar that you can see and hear and touch with your own hands: making lists, paying old or neglected debts, taking daily moments of quiet time during which you stop all activity, being honest when evasion seems easier, telling your story, and listening to others tell theirs.

The more mystical aspects of a spiritual life rise from this foundation—not by decision or hard work, but by a less rational process, perhaps in response to the readiness of your foundation. The rock foundation for a house makes a durable base for a home. No one can force happiness in a home or force a spiritually good life. But you can lay one stone upon another to build a solid foundation, and that makes the next part more possible.

The practice of the Serenity Prayer is another part of the foundation: "God grant me the serenity to accept the things I cannot change, the courage to change the things I can, and the wisdom to know the difference." Commonly used at meetings, this prayer teaches this valuable distinction: wisdom to see what you can control and to work at it, and acceptance of what you cannot control.

The Eighth and Ninth Steps suggest concrete, deliberate actions. In the Eighth you take pencil and paper and make a list of the names of people you have harmed. In the Ninth you actually make amends to those people.

The goals of these two Steps are your own peace of mind and relief from shame and guilt. They may seem like big challenges. They may look like they will force you into embarrassing positions. It is true that they might be difficult for you, yet you will not have to do anything you are not ready to do. No action should be forced before you are ready. The work of making your list and making direct amends may be very difficult for you. But it comes when the time seems right. Your higher power will guide you.

A long-time member of ACOA reflected on the Steps this way:

> Many of us have lived in families that shamed and abused or discounted us whenever there was an opening. Admitting a mistake in such a system always invited others to dump their blame and shame on our heads. So our need for self-defense drew us away from honesty and away from connection with our true selves. Now, to make the list of Step Eight or to deal honestly with the people we have harmed may seem dangerously vulnerable; may raise profound feelings of shame and guilt exactly as we were conditioned to feel; and may bring forth loud inner voices that desperately justify our actions so we can avoid doing the Step. By not doing it we might avoid that old conditioned shame reaction, but we also miss the benefit of feeling grown-up and clear.

You can approach the Step gently. For example, Andrew settled into his window seat in row eight for his business flight to Detroit and thought, *Why does the number eight have to come up again right away this morning?* His Codependents of Sex Addicts (COSA) meeting the night before was on Step Eight, and he felt unsettled by it. He had been going to meetings for almost a year and life had improved remarkably. It had been a rolling crisis until he and his wife got into marriage therapy and their therapist directed them into Twelve Step groups. Life had changed in ways that felt miraculous, and he didn't want to rock the boat by digging into the past.

On the one hand, he felt he had not been honest with anyone and had misled them all because he had not been honest with himself. He had kept the secret about his wife's affairs for so long that he felt like a liar. He also felt the pain of his nights alone when he had kept "a stiff upper lip" and held in his feelings. On the other hand, he felt that he had done the best he could with what he had and that no one could expect anything more.

But the woman in his meeting who talked about her work on Step Eight said something that told him it was time to begin. He couldn't sit still forever just to hold onto his calm feelings. She said, "I didn't really have my integrity. Even when things were better, I still just reacted most of the time to whatever came into my life until I went back to clean up some of my old messes."

He sat in the airplane seat, aware of the spiral notebook now by his feet. He had stuffed it into his briefcase as he packed the night before. While hating to unearth the past, he began considering names that might go on the list of people he had harmed. He would waver between putting everyone he ever knew on the list and putting no one on it. But the speaker at the meeting said it helped her to simply go into action and push past her mental debates. She put a pencil in her hand and wrote names as they came to mind without sifting and screening them for final decisions. She just called it her tentative list and knew she would add and subtract names as she thought more about them later.

Andrew knew that his reluctance came largely from remembering his own behavior while his wife was in the most extreme stage of her addiction. He had been dishonest with her. He had often spent money on things such as a new camper and a new stereo system when they had agreed to save for other things. He didn't let her see his anger directly, but instead took it out on her by "forgetting" her birthday and by making jokes at her expense when she fell and broke her arm. Amends now would only open that can of worms. He didn't even want to think about it.

Andrew got to his hotel room in the evening after a day of work and sat down with his notebook. He immediately put his wife at the top of his list, and without further reflection he went on to other people about whom he felt regrets. He included the owner of the hardware store, where on Saturday he had slipped a new pair of pliers into his pocket without paying. He stopped after writing "Myself" on the page. He felt completed with his list and surprised at how quickly it was done. That night as he was brushing his teeth and getting ready for bed he looked in the mirror and realized, *Tonight I treated my conscience with new respect. I took the muzzle off my inner voice.* As he lay in bed before he fell asleep, he felt personal power and authority fill his body. And he knew no one could ever take that away.

Step Eight: Made a list of all persons we had harmed, and became willing to make amends to them all.

A clear separation between Steps Eight and Nine will help you get going. Step Eight is your own private list, and you have complete control over who you put on it and who you take off. When you put someone on your list, no further action is required at that time. It means only that you can honestly admit to yourself that your actions caused someone harm. You may not feel ready to do anything about it. This Step helps you with your lack of readiness. Repair comes in Step Nine, if at all, and nowhere is it written that you have to meet any timetable in getting ready.

How do you know who to put on your list? "You Always Hurt the One You Love" is a song title that speaks the truth. You cannot be a member of a family or live with someone without hurting him at times. You may not mean to do anyone harm. A relationship is like a house that constantly needs upkeep and repair. You may want to help a loved one or protect him, but your actions have a disrespectful or undermining effect. Certainly there are times when you have been so angry that you did something hurtful, or maybe you have been sneaky, thoughtless, self-centered, or impulsive. Remember to put yourself on your list. You may have been the one most injured, most frustrated, and most stymied by your codependent outlook and conditioning. The golden rule, "Treat others as you would like them to treat you," can guide you in deciding whether someone belongs on your list.

Perhaps as you write a particular name, you know immediately how and when to make amends. With another name you may only know that you caused that person harm, but how to make amends, if ever, may be completely puzzling. That's okay for Step Eight. Some names may stay on your list for a very long time as you wait to become ready. Sometimes a change in circumstances creates a possibility, sometimes you need to get stronger within. Sometimes you get the peacefulness of feeling ready within, but the opportunity or appropriate time doesn't occur for a while. When the time does come, however, you will be ready to respond.

Step Nine: Made direct amends to such people wherever possible, except when to do so would injure them or others.

Step Nine suggests that you take action when you are ready to correct your wrongs with the people on your list.

This Step confronts shame directly. Shame is the feeling of a dead-end with no possibility of repair and no way back. This Step counters shame by affirming a way back, by making genuine amends in the real world. Many people get stuck in their growth because they are convinced of their shame. They believe that there is no repair for their wrongs; they feel hopeless and even defiant about trying. By asserting yourself to make amends, you assert your rightful place as an equal member of the human race—no less and no greater than all other people.

You are cautioned against taking actions in the name of honesty that can cause further harm. One man went home after a meeting and decided to unburden his guilty conscience about betraying his former friend. So he impulsively called the friend he hadn't seen in months and told him that he had had an affair with his wife two years earlier. Revealing such a secret to his friend intruded on that marriage in a brash, sudden, and destructive way. If he had talked it over with another friend first he might have seen that he was not making amends at all. Reflection, a sense of timing and patience, and the counseling of trusted friends in the program or with a sponsor are vital to this Step.

A good example of making direct amends comes from Andrew's way of dealing with the hardware store where he stole the pliers. After talking with others in his COSA group, he eventually walked into the store with money in hand for the cost of the pliers.

He said to the owner, "I walked out of here with a pair of pliers three years ago without paying for them and I feel bad about it. I want to pay what I owe you. So here's the money." One friend had suggested to Andrew that rather than going in person to the store, he could write an anonymous letter with the cash enclosed. That might have been an acceptable way, but for Andrew, *direct amends* meant he would do it face to face. He was relieved that the store owner was glad to get the money and said to him, "I've got to pat you on the back for coming in here with it. I respect you for your courage, and I hope you will continue to be my customer."

Ingredients of a Genuine Apology

In working on Step Nine, keep in mind the ingredients of a real apology. They include (1) naming specifically what you did that you regret, something that you are willing to be responsible for, (2) saying you are sorry, and (3) listening to the other person's responses. It might include saying you can see how the other person could be angry at your actions. Keep in mind that feeling guilty and repairing your mistakes is about your *behavior,* not about you as a person.

Apology is difficult, but it doesn't require your humiliation or self-denigration. Shame only distracts you from the repair you have set out to do. Interestingly, the Hebrew word for sin translates into "missing the mark." Your actions were off-target. Making amends acknowledges the truth and takes responsibility for the consequences without the sackcloth and ashes.

Conversely, an apology that starts with, "If I did anything that hurt you. . . " or "If I did something wrong. . . " doesn't name anything you did to regret, so your genuine apology is aborted. That can be a signal to you that you are manipulating your language so that you appear apologetic without delivering the real McCoy. Similarly, "I'm sorry you felt bad. . . " or "I'm sorry you took it the wrong way. . . " are not apologies for your behavior, since they shift the focus to the other person. They only say that you regret the way the other person responded. You can also take back an apology while giving it when you say things like, "Nobody's perfect!" and "I'm sorry, but if it weren't for what you did first I never would have. . . ."

Your amends list may include names of people who are no

longer alive, or people who would be more harmed by your admission than by your original deed. You will not grow from unburdening yourself of tension and guilt when it only leaves others feeling worse.

Your creative mind and the inspiration of your higher power come into play to determine less direct ways to make amends. One belief among those in the program is that the improved, more thoughtful, spiritual life you now live constitutes reparation for past wrongs. For example, parents who regret mistakes they made with their children can genuinely live their Ninth Step today by being more conscious and faithful in their current relationships with their children, no matter what their ages. Volunteering to help with neighborhood cleanup day might symbolically make amends for things you can't repair directly.

Actions for Your Eighth and Ninth Steps

Make a list of old important relationships that have drifted away or ended in anger. Do some of them belong on your Eighth Step list? Perhaps you have cut off relationships with friends or relatives because you were not willing to face your mistakes. You may not have wanted to say how much you covered up for someone else's craziness. Feelings of shame often lead people to go away because they don't see repair as being possible.

When your thoughts are clear and you are ready to make amends to someone, you may still be unsure of how to go about it and afraid of how that person will respond. That is a good time to *sit down with a trusted friend and role-play the conversation first.* Say what you have to say as if your friend were the real person you are making amends to, and ask your friend to respond in the role of the other person. Tell your friend what your fears are, and play out the reactions you are afraid of. That way you can actually work through several possibilities and get ready to say and do what you most want to say and do.

Think of a time in your past when you did something or accomplished a task that you deeply respected. It might have been a job you weren't sure you could do, or something you had put off for a long time because you dreaded it, but when you finally did it you felt good. As you think about that time, use it as a marker, a memory that can guide you to where you are going in Steps Eight and Nine.

I am present for others. I let others see the real me.

CHAPTER SEVEN

Every person is an aristocrat.
Every human is noble and of royal blood,
born from the intimate depths of the divine nature
and the divine wilderness.

—Meister Eckhart

Becoming Visible Persons: Living in the Present

Step Ten: *Continued to take personal inventory and when we were wrong promptly admitted it.*

Step Eleven: *Sought through prayer and meditation to improve our conscious contact with* god as we understood god, *praying only for knowledge of god's will for us and the power to carry that out.*

Step Twelve: *Having had a spiritual awakening as the result of these steps, we tried to carry this message to others, and to practice these principles in all our affairs.*[1]

*B*efore people begin a recovery program, they're carrying around a lot of duties, obligations, and personality quirks because they think they have to. They might be seen as a group of backpackers hiking in the mountains, weighted down with backpacks, layers of sweaters and jackets, rain gear, sleeping bags, and Stetson hats, with camping cups, Swiss Army knives, and even cameras dangling from their packs and belts. As they move along the trail, they look lumpy, bulky, misshapen. They all look alike. The natural shape of their individual bodies is difficult to detect under all that gear. But when it's time to stop to make camp the hikers set their gear down, take off all the layers, and stretch their arms in the sun. Then you see the natural shape of the body, and the personality of each comes alive, separate from the group.

Even so, as people in the program do their work, their behaviors change, and certain habits fall away. It's as though they've dropped off unnecessary burdens—they're carrying less baggage—and consequently their personalities become more visible. For example, as Laura L. spent less time obsessing about her partner's behavior by working Steps Six through Nine, she discovered she suddenly had time. Time! Nobody told her the program would give her more time. Maybe it didn't really give her time, but she suddenly had the emotional energy to feel as if she could take the time to do more in her life. She took up her old hobby of woodworking. She refinished an oak table and built new bookshelves for the TV room. Not only did her skill become more evident to herself and other people, but she also had the visible evidence of having a place in the world other than that of her relationship.

Interestingly, what often happens is that as people change on the inside, they also change on the outside. People notice them more. Laura slowly got stronger as she did her physical work. She also became more visible because she walked with more authority.

Steps Six through Nine allow behaviors to change. As behaviors change, people become more individual and visible to the world and to themselves.

As people become more visible, the last three Steps are the way that people maintain their program. The last three Steps are the method for processing the previous lessons on a daily basis.

Step Ten: Continued to take personal inventory and when we were wrong promptly admitted it.

The word *continued* is such a magical word. It implies movement, change, timelessness. French philosopher and mathematician Blaise Pascal said, "Our nature lies in movement; complete calm is death." Life continues, human growth continues. The word *continued* is reassurance that the recovery process is good.

Some people think that the word *continued* means "on a daily basis." Others look at the Step in a looser fashion and say that the general idea is for a person to make a commitment to some kind of self-monitoring. It might be a checklist, it might be a list of questions. It might be writing in a journal every night before bed. It might be calling a friend once a week. Somehow, though, there's the idea of a reality check, an evaluation, or an inventory that surveys the character defects you'd like to let go of.

The phrase *promptly admitted it* is a call to process life more quickly than before you were in the program. If you've made a mistake, don't get hung up on guilt and shame; rather, face what you've done, and make amends. If you stay conscious of this immediate processing, then the need for a lengthy Step Four does not come up for a long time. The word *admitted* in Step Ten always throws you back to Step One and the basic human powerlessness to control life, god, and other people. The symmetry of Steps One and Ten is pleasing to contemplate. The word *promptly* gives you permission to be honest faster than you were before. *Promptly* is a relief for people who have spent years holding back from speaking their own thoughts and feelings, years of trying to find the words to be honest. *Promptly* gives permission for your life to be an adventure, the adventure of honesty, being true to yourself on your journey. The immediacy of prompt self-expression gives a sense of adventure to living, to letting your feelings flow.

When you're new to the program, the Step Ten inventory may consist of a checklist of negative behaviors you'd like to avoid, what some might even call "obnoxious" behaviors. But after a while, Step Ten may seem like a continuing and deeper process; rather than looking for the negative, a person may ask, *What is it I'm not doing that I could be doing?* For example, one woman asks every morning, *How am I holding back from myself?* Because this question is open-ended, the answers vary. Sometimes a voice comes to her, softly, with *You need to let yourself enjoy that wonderful dream about skiing and the blue light reflecting off the snow.* Sometimes the voice is more practical, saying *Mail the job application.*

Actions for Your Tenth Step:
How Am I Holding Back from Myself?

Step Ten work may involve a general question that you ask yourself every morning to use as a rudder for sailing through the day. You may also do an inventory at night as you think over the day's work and pleasure. Each evening, you may review your activities of the day. How did you feel as you did them? What do your feelings tell you?

What questions could help you focus on your own development?

- How am I holding back from myself?
- How can I be more visible to myself?
- How can *I* come forward today?

Here are some suggestions about holding back, being visible, coming forward.

Bring Back Lost Parts of the Self

One way of holding back is by not reclaiming lost parts of yourself that you want to have in your life. What qualities did you once have that you could reclaim? Relaxing by taking a dance class? Visiting your best friend from high school? What qualities have you not developed that you wish you could develop? You might think about all the dreams you had for yourself when you were young. Many aspects of the self are left undeveloped in the normal process of growing up. Additionally, caretaking causes neglect of the self. What can you do to reclaim one lost part of yourself?

Let Go of the Past

Another way of holding back is by trying to hang on to something lost that can't be reclaimed. Sometimes people unconsciously hold on to the *idea* of a relationship that is long gone. For example, one woman in Al-Anon discovered that she was still holding on to the dream that her ex-husband would become a good father, that her children would have two functioning parents. They had been divorced for fifteen years and they were both now in their second marriages. She had no thoughts of reconciling with him, yet she wanted him to be a father to their children.

When they were married, he had been physically abusive and had beat her up many times, sometimes in the presence of the children. He blamed his battering on his drinking. She must have bought into this idea, because once he got sober she thought his other behaviors would also change. She suddenly realized she had been in denial when she received a letter from him accusing her of having affairs twenty-five years earlier. The tone had the emotional intensity of someone who was wronged yesterday. She was horrified—this man is mentally ill, she realized. He was still hooked on being right, on controlling her reality. His thought processes were frightening. She realized she had to stop communicating with him about their children—-about anything. It was time for the divorce to be final in an emotional sense. She sent his letter back to him with a note:

> This is not my reality. I don't want this letter in my house.
>
> I don't want to tear this letter up in resentment or anger and so I am sending it back to you.
>
> Any letters that arrive with your postmark will be opened and read by someone else, not by me.

She asked a friend to be with her when she sealed the letter. They said "good-bye" to the man who had been in her life for so many years. She felt a deep sadness that he could not be what she wanted. But it was time to let go, to feel her sadness. She had released herself from her connection to him. She knew she would never read another letter from him. This was a real ending for her.

Let Go of Internalized Images of Diminishment

This recovery program is about learning that it's okay to be visible. To have outlines. To have opinions. To have a unique personal history.

If you have lived your life in the service of what the world wants you to be, it may be that the world has given you negative labels about who you are. You must discover these labels and release them. Our culture gives negative labels to people of color, to women, to those in minority religions, to the disabled, to gay men and lesbians, and to those who don't fit in for other reasons— young boys for being sissies, artists, and so on. Some people were teased mercilessly when they were children. Some common belittling names include fatso, clumsy, ugly, stupid. It seems as if *most* people have received some negative information about themselves. In addition, if you grew up in a shaming family, you may have been told that you're not good enough in a hundred different ways.

How have you been diminished? If you were to stop reading this now, open your front door, and sing out to the neighborhood, "I'm a good enough person just the way I am," how would the voices inside your head answer you? *Stop calling attention to yourself! Stop being so contrary!* When you look in the mirror in the morning and sing out, "I'm good enough," what does the mirror say back? Yes, you are? No, you're too dark, too girlish, too fat, too little, too weird? It's time to let go of these negative labels.

Becoming more visible means that you take responsibility for growing, for *continuing* with your life. This responsibility entails affirming that you are good enough the way you are; it also entails actively working to let go of the negative feelings and images you carry inside you, the lost parts that will never be, and the negative labels that were never true. As you work on releasing the negativism, your unconscious will probably also release memories of things you've done that you feel guilty about, perhaps in reaction to these labels. It is okay to identify these hurtful behaviors, your irresponsible actions, and become accountable for them. You have a right to be imperfect and to work on changing.

Step Eleven: Sought through prayer and meditation to improve our conscious contact with **god as we understood god,** *praying only for knowledge of god's will for us and the power to carry that out.*

The word *sought* is another word for "searched." When you search, you are moving. *Sought* has the same sense of growing and changing as the word *continued.*

So in this Step the idea of continuing is linked to the idea of prayer and meditation, which are a continuing part of a person's spiritual work. A daily practice is a common manifestation of this Step.

How do people actually practice prayer and meditation? Because of the diversity of people in Twelve Step programs, there is a wide interpretation of this Step. Some people follow a traditional form of prayer that comes from an established religion, such as going to mass or taking time for the discipline of meditation taught by Eastern religions.

People who have been disillusioned with established religions also maintain a continuing practice of meditation and prayer. Some people in the program are not at ease using the word *god*, but prayer and meditation have given them a connection to other people and a sense of belonging. Meditation has changed them so that they now feel at home in the universe.

Here are some suggestions on how you could interpret these two words in nonreligious terms:

- Prayer is focusing on what you'd like to see come into being in your life and into the world.
- Meditation is the practice of letting go and listening. It means taking time to quiet the mind.

This Step directs the nature of prayer by saying, "praying only for god's will and the power to carry that out." This direction to pray for *only* god's will sends prayers back to the realm of listening, to meditation, to being in the presence of the spirit, waiting to discover what is to be done. Stop doing, stop fixing, and start listening. Again, an important message here is simply to *be.*

Sometimes people have trouble comprehending what god's will is for their lives, even though they are taking time for silence and following their program. That means they are in a wintering of the spirit, a period of waiting, of being empty. This is a spiritual state that needs to be respected as much as the times that are clear and joyful.

At other times people have a sense of god's will and struggle with the last phrase of the Step, "the power to carry that out."

A man in Al-Anon says he believes it is god's will for him to be calm, yet he doubts his power to carry it out. In addition to recovering from codependency, he lives with a chronic illness and is often anxiety-ridden. He practices the Step through listening to relaxation tapes and saying affirmations. He repeats his affirmations over and over throughout the day:

- I release this anxiety to god's light and love.
- I rest in the calm of god's love.

He says, "I had to keep saying the same thing over and over until it finally took. I mean it literally, that I kept repeating certain affirmations over and over. It took a long time to sink into my bones." He says that the practice of meditation and prayer brings the abstract idea of god's will into the physical reality of his life, into his body, feelings, and consciousness:

> When I start to have an anxiety attack, I go back into my practice of prayer and repetition. As they say in my

meeting, "It works if you work it." I think what finally worked was that I surrendered to my illness, I surrendered to my divorce. I prayed only for calmness in the moment. I gave up all prayer for outcomes. I lived into each moment of my life.

Like this man, if you have internal resistance to what you believe is god's will, you may be receiving, through your resistance, an additional message that you're on the right track. Internal resistance may also be an indication of the powerful hold that negative beliefs have on your mind. Negativity always fights back. As Brenda Schaeffer writes, "To the unconscious mind, addictive love makes perfect sense; it feels necessary to survival itself."[2] Affirmations work on the conscious and unconscious level to combat your negative beliefs.

Not everyone, however, likes to practice affirmations. As we said earlier, some people use this Step to direct themselves to more traditional practices. One woman writes down a few quotations from sacred writings and contemporary writers that are guides for where she is at any particular time. She says she "sits with the quotes" and lets their meaning come into her.

However you choose to practice this Step, it is always about living in the moment, living in present time, living in your present reality. It is about giving up what you thought you wanted and finding in your heart acceptance of life situations that are difficult to accept. This Step is the tool by which acceptance can become a reality on a daily basis. It's for people who face the loss of a partner and the dream of their family being together. It's for finding the strength to combat the negative beliefs that have their hold on you. It's for facing illness, death, loss, and tragedy.

This Step is also for facing positive changes and accepting that you have the right to enjoy the good things that come your way. It's for feeling good about your life even if there are no outer changes—no fame, no fortune, no melodrama.

The work you do on this Step may also manifest itself as a call for you to take action in the world against social injustice, to work for the welfare of other people. This Step is the foundation from which you are empowered to go into the world and take a stand on political issues. You are grounded in your connection to your .higher power.

This Step is about acceptance of your life as it is. The writer Tony Hillerman often includes in his mysteries the beliefs of the Navajo people. One of our favorite quotations is in synch with the work and purpose of this Step: "You stay in harmony with reality."[3]

Whatever your life situation, this Step brings you the promise of being in harmony, of being fully alive in the moment, of being in conscious contact with your higher power. As you surrender to this Step, you are letting yourself become more and more visible as a child of the universe.

Actions for Your Eleventh Step

Find a notebook and do some free writing to explore the times you have felt *conscious contact*—you may be surprised at what you discover. Some people have the most solitude and experience the most powerful sense of a spiritual presence when they are driving on the freeway. Others may feel centered in a particular room of their house, or in a religious sanctuary. After you have explored the times you've been most conscious of your higher power, think about how you could improve the possibilities of this happening again. Do you need to set aside time for solitude or for another meeting? Do you need to put on a special tape or just turn off the radio? Many people say they need to be outside to feel the spirit, the conscious contact. What would have to happen in your life for you to be outside more?

Buy a special notebook to be your continuing-prayer notebook. You could use this notebook to center your thoughts and feelings each day. Many people in the program keep a prayer list, people they want to remember and pray for in their meditation time. This list may include people from the work done in Steps Eight and Nine. It may also include people for whom you want to send prayers of gratitude and thanks. We know one person who writes one prayer at bedtime. After a year, there's a prayer for every day. Writing a new prayer every day is both a focusing experience on life as it happens and a record of the year's journey.

Many people use dreams and unconscious connections to images of spirituality as a means for becoming conscious. You can write down your dreams and be with them to understand them.

You can read about many gods and goddesses and people whose spirit you want somehow to grow into . . . the aspect of the spiritual that you need at any given time.

You may want to read and write for your journey and for this Step. If you are a more physical person, you may want to go and sit by a lake and look at the stars. You may want to make an altar in your house or garden. One man made a centering place in his garden out of his stones and other objects he found in nature. You may make one place that is your centering place, such as one special table with pictures and candles and beloved objects. Or you may know that a particular room is the place where you feel whole, and you can make a special commitment to keeping it clean and orderly or in whatever way gives you a sense of peace. Cleaning, lighting candles, gardening, walking, dancing, listening to music, looking at the stars can all be considered acts of prayer.

By reading, writing, and physical action, you express your harmony with reality.

Prayer and meditation offer the conscious contact of belonging to the universe, of having a place in the larger scheme of things. Here is a beautiful poem that expresses this belonging:

WILD GEESE

You do not have to be good.
You do not have to walk on your knees
for a hundred miles through the desert, repenting.
You only have to let the soft animal of your body love
    what it loves.
Tell me about despair, yours, and I will tell you mine.
Meanwhile the world goes on.
Meanwhile the sun and the clear pebbles of the rain
are moving across the landscapes,
over the prairies and the deep trees,
the mountains and the rivers.
Meanwhile the wild geese, high in the clean blue air,
are heading home.
Whoever you are, no matter how lonely,
the world offers itself to your imagination,

calls to you like the wild geese, harsh and exciting—
over and over announcing your place
in the family of things.

—Mary Oliver

Step Twelve: Having had a spiritual awakening as the result of these steps, we tried to carry this message to others, and to practice these principles in all our affairs.

The substance of this Step is acknowledgment of a spiritual awakening. A spiritual awakening is usually not a conversion with Fourth of July fireworks and a marching band. And it is not a continuing sense of high. In fact, the Step doesn't say that we in the program are *awake*. It says that people have had an *awakening*. Some days are more awake than others. Having had a glimmer of what the spirit is all about, people go about their daily work more or less conscious of the spirit.

People in the program describe their awakenings in many different ways. Here's a sampling of what the phrase *spiritual awakening* means to some:

> The change in my life came out of crisis. It was that summer at the cabin. I had horrible nightmares, living hallucinations. Before that time, I wore the mask of health but it shattered. The more that I could become was pushing out. I think of the grass growing up in the cracks of the sidewalk, that strength. I resisted. I was set in my ways. But when I crashed, I realized that whatever force it was, it wants everything to grow, including me. It was the life force. I couldn't resist it. I could trust it. It would carry me, it would support me. I was going to become more.

* * * * *

> I'm able to enjoy the small pleasures in life. There's a new word with the chemical dependency counselors—*anhedonia*. They started using it about cocaine addicts. Anhedonia means *the inability to experience pleasure.* I don't know why they don't use it for us, those of us all twisted up with codependency. Everybody I've

met in my situation has been cut off from physical pleasures. I am slowly regaining my connection to daily life, to the normal pleasures of being glad to wake up in the morning, to see the sun, to smell the toast, to read the paper. My spiritual awakening is my resurrection to the ordinary morning.

* * * * *

One day I felt like my molecules had rearranged themselves. I realized I didn't want to put up with getting pushed around anymore. I changed the rules in my family. Just like that. In one day I made enormous changes I'd been inching toward for years. Our therapist looked at me and said, "What's come over you?" All I could think to say was, "Life's too short. I'm tired of waiting around for *my* life to begin." And so it did.

* * * * *

I'm an alcoholic, but all that drinking helped me be a really great codependent husband too. When I got sober I didn't ever want to get high again. I was scared to death, relieved to get that monkey off my back. . . . No more highs for me. No more peak experiences. I don't relate to the words "higher power." When I started to let go of my codependency in my sobriety I thought: what I need in my life is lower power, energy that keeps me low to the ground, where I can lie low, be centered, grounded. That power came to me. I'm happy for the first time in my life.

* * * * *

The day of my spiritual awakening was the May Day Parade in 1984. I was there with my family. They all drifted off to do other things, see people, sign petitions, buy Sno-Cones, dance, smoke a cigarette without getting noticed. I was sitting alone. It occurred to me that in the past I would've thought I had to get up and *do something,* not sit there where anybody could see me sitting alone. I didn't pretend to be having fun. I didn't get up and go look for people I knew, although I'd seen maybe fourteen people go by who I did know. I didn't paste a smile on my face. I sat in the sun and relaxed. I was overwhelmed with a mild yet powerful feeling of being connected to everyone there, without having to do anything to demonstrate that feeling of connection. And even if I had been there all alone, not planted on the family blanket for my family to find me again, I would've still felt that sense of belonging. It was a first, and I mark the day as the beginning of my spiritual awakening. Now when I go into a crowd of people, I can be me, whatever else is happening, without apology for who I am, without bragging, without hiding who I am.

*   *   *   *   *

I once thought that if I found the courage to come out as a lesbian I would be at peace, even if I had problems with others' homophobia, because I would be going out into the world as my real self. Coming out *was* a great relief. But I was still restless in the spirit. When my partner went into treatment, I went to Al-Anon because the treatment counselors told me to. What a shock to discover that it had something for *me.* As I've learned to let go of controlling our relationship, I've let go of a lot of fear and worry about the world in general. I'm at peace with myself and the world. My spiritual awakening came in through the chimney or the back door when I wasn't looking.

*   *   *   *   *

I didn't feel alive unless I was in a relationship. I thought I was an okay person, but I didn't feel *alive* without that buzz. It was like I was a Christmas tree, decorated but waiting for that special someone to plug in the lights. I gave it up. I picture myself as a pine tree in the woods, in the middle of winter, surrounded by snow. It's not lonely. I like snow. It's peaceful, the sounds are different. But I miss the charge of the electricity. I have to hold on to the picture of the winter pine tree. Slowly that pine tree is becoming the one I want to be.

* * * * *

What do all of these experiences have in common? They all share the powerful feeling of belonging in the world, in the community of human beings. They also share that absolute sense of assurance that your well-being doesn't depend on the outcome of your present human relationships. Whatever happens, you'll be okay.

A spiritual awakening means that you are good enough as you are. Like the person at the May Day Parade, when you go out in the world, you get to be present in the moment, you get to be visible without fear, without shame, without false pride. You get to be who you are.

A spiritual awakening means that your sanity does not depend on your relationships with other people. You are no longer dependent on the approval of your partner or your family or friends for your well-being. No matter what happens with all your friends and family, there will be love for you in the universe. A spiritual awakening means that even if you grew up in a troubled family, and even if you have been abandoned and abused, you can actually face the world without parents and know that you will still find love in the universe. A spiritual awakening means that if you have in the past been dependent on falling in love to feel alive, you can not only survive without a lover, but you can also learn to trust (and believe) that love is present for you without the addictive high. And even if your children go away, even if your friends abandon you, you will still receive love from the universe. In some way it will come to you. A spiritual awakening means you live as if you are loved.

By living the Twelve Steps, you learn to carry serenity within you. When you go out into the world, you feel centered. You are in touch with a spiritual place within you every day, which you previously may have experienced only on special occasions, like a hiking trip into the Sierra mountains, a vacation in Mexico, or going to a concert. You may feel this spirituality resonate through the universe.

And so when you move on to the rest of Step Twelve, you move from the place of being loved and accepted to the place of being present for other people. By being present to your own life, you are able to be present to other people.

To carry the message to others means first that you stay centered in your own life and act in a trustworthy manner in all aspects of your life. As in some other Steps, the message here is to *be*. You may have been so busy doing for others that you have not had presence of mind to simply *be* with them. Now that you are on the recovery path, you can tell your story, connect with other people, and keep your own boundaries. You don't have to be overwhelmed by the suffering of others, and you don't have to be in charge of fixing their lives. You can simply be on the journey together. You can now be in mutually caring relationships with appropriate nurturing and kindness. Being with other people is something that is deeply satisfying, a joyful experience to look forward to every morning.

Actions for Your Twelfth Step

Call a friend and tell the story of your spiritual awakening.

Or go to a meeting and reflect on how your life has changed.

To encourage a strong sense of self, you might keep as a role model one other human who walks in the world with self-assurance. The artist Pitseolak is a Native American born on Nottingham Island in Hudson Bay. When she was a child, her people were living in the old ways. After the invasion of Western civilization, she made drawings and prints of sea pigeons, people, sealskin boats, that have brought her great acclaim. She has great self-assurance about her life and her drawings:

> I am going to keep on doing them . . . I shall make them as long as I am well. If I can, I'll make them even after I'm dead.[4]

The Steps Bring You Full Circle

As you come to the end of this chapter on Step Twelve, you may have the sensation of coming full circle, of returning to Step One, for inherent in this Step is a letting go that may bring with it the terror of utter powerlessness over other people and

101

relationships. From terror to trust. That moves Step Twelve back to Step One. You may have a physical sensation of movement.

Working the Steps gives you a sense of walking, of journey, of moving and being moved. Sometimes as we're writing, as authors, we forget the literal meaning of the word *step*. The Steps are stages on a journey, in a spiral process, but the word *step* most of all refers to the act of walking. The movement through the steps is one meaning of the Steps. The more you walk, the more you understand the walk.

In the book *The Songlines*, Bruce Chatwin describes the many spiritual traditions that present the idea of walking into the meaning; the person who is walking is the embodiment of the message. In Islam, for example, especially among the Sufis, the action of walking is used to detach from the world. Buddha is reported to have said, "You cannot travel on the path before you have become the Path itself." The journey is the message.

Walking with other people as a peer is in and of itself an essential part of the process of the Twelve Steps. Walking and talking together is one way of describing the phrase "carry the message." By being with other people, by becoming vulnerable enough to share the story of your own process and recovery, by listening to the stories of others, you are carrying the message. You walk through the Steps with others on the path you share.

Be present to yourself. Be present to others. Walk on.

SECTION THREE:

SEEING THE WORLD
WITH NEW EYES

I trust the quiet transformation.

CHAPTER EIGHT

You must give birth to your images.
They are the future waiting to be born . . .
fear not the strangeness you feel. The future must
enter into you long before it happens. . . . Just wait
for the birth . . . for the hour of new clarity.
—Rainer Maria Rilke

Trusting the Mystery Of Transformation

Now we've completed our look at each of the Twelve Steps. We've talked about how you can work on them and how each one advances your recovery. Here we want to talk about another important dynamic; that is, how the Twelve Step program *as a whole* works for you.

The Steps work together to create a combined effect, greater than the sum of the individual parts. There is a word for this process—*synergy.* The term *synergistic effect* refers to events that you can explain only when you see how separate forces cooperate and combine to make something new. For example, we talked about the First Step as being the *surrender* Step, the Second the *belief* Step, the Third the *relationship* Step, and so on. But those who go beyond the work and impact of each Step and follow them as a continuous circle in their lives undergo a transformation in outlook and personality that reaches beyond anything they've worked on. Recovering people who notice such change in themselves and each other often feel it as a miracle because they never expected it; it seems like a gift.

David Berenson says the word *transformation* means a "radical" shift "in one's view of what is real." It may happen intensely and suddenly, but it usually occurs gradually. Transformation is different from a *peak experience*, which may be a profound emotional event but doesn't have a lasting effect. Nor is it a *conversion experience,* which is a turn toward a dogma or religious belief to explain experiences.[1]

This program requires hard work, risk, and your willingness to face pain. Yet, as one man said about his good baseball pitching performance, "You can't force it, you can't put it there, it has to come." The change called transformation is like that. It often seems to come without effort, perhaps without your even knowing it happened. You have worked at the program and done what the Steps suggest. But your work is on specific parts as laid out in the Steps, and your transformation goes above and beyond the parts you worked on. It is a change in your personality. This change comes more as a result of the whole set of Steps and has a surprise aspect as spiritual things sometimes do. You work at the Steps in this program, but you can't work at transformation. Your work on the Steps makes you ready to receive the transformation that comes.

The original book *Alcoholics Anonymous,* first published in 1939, spells out the Twelve Steps newly developed by the first emerging group of recovering alcoholics. It uses the terms *spiritual experience* and *spiritual awakening* many times throughout, and says that they refer to the "personality change sufficient to bring recovery from alcoholism."[2] The changes may come very suddenly, but most "develop slowly over a period of time. . . . Our members find that they have tapped an unsuspected inner source which they presently identify with their own conception of a Power greater than themselves."[3]

We know a woman named Janeen who lives in California. She had several years of roller-coaster mood swings that came from recurring crises in her relationships. She saw the pattern herself and told a friend, "I've come to think that even when I feel good, it's just the top of the wave before everything crashes around me again." Janeen's boyfriend's life had a similar boom-and-bust cycle as he rode the addictive spending wave. When Dan had a few dollars to spend or a credit card that was below its credit limit, he could buy expensive shoes and shirts and suddenly felt like a strong, successful man. But the downside of the wave always brought abusive phone calls from collection people, eviction notices for unpaid rent, reclaimed merchandise, and court orders to pay bills.

Janeen always believed that better times were just around the corner. She saw the good person in Dan who came out when they were alone and when he was in his better moments. So she would "lend" him money to bail him out of his crises, thinking that when he got on his feet he would surely pay her back. She often went shopping with him, feeling the rising tension in the air between them as she tried to provide the limits that he didn't have. They spent hours together in shopping malls even though she didn't enjoy it; but she thought if she stayed by his side she could reduce his impulsive buying. She became financially strapped herself from all the crises she quelled with her paycheck and finally started her own "secret" account to help her feel secure.

He entered the Spenders Anonymous program and after several weeks suggested that Janeen go to S-Anon, a program for people in a relationship with an addictive spender. She quickly got active in that program, just as she always did with any project in her life. She went to weekly meetings, made friends with others in the group, and found they had amazingly similar stories. She read hungrily about the Steps and worked to do what they suggested.

Janeen correctly assumed that if she devoted herself to it, she would get more benefits from the program than if she just casually attended weekly meetings to absorb what she could. But she didn't know that there isn't always a direct correlation between the specific points you work on and the benefits you receive. When she first worked on releasing her frenzied attempts to control Dan's spending, she hoped to improve her relationship with him and get him to feel more responsible.

But she was surprised by her new feelings of inner calm and her greater ability to concentrate despite how things were going with Dan. Her friends told her that in some intangible way she was more present in conversations and easier to talk with, and her sales production climbed at work. Her supervisor said in her evaluation conference, "I don't know what you're doing differently, Janeen, but whatever it is, keep on doing it!" After two years, her life was so different that her relationship with Dan wasn't even the point of her involvement in S-Anon.

In *Alcoholics Anonymous*, commonly called "The Big Book," a paragraph about the benefits of this program describes personality changes that are familiar to those who live closely by the Steps. These benefits are referred to as "the promises."

> If we are painstaking about this phase of our development, we will be amazed before we are half way through. We are going to know a new freedom and a new happiness. We will not regret the past nor wish to shut the door on it. We will comprehend the word serenity and we will know peace. No matter how far down the scale we have gone, we will see how our experience can benefit others. That feeling of uselessness and self-pity will disappear. We will lose interest in selfish things and gain interest in our fellows. Self-seeking will slip away. Our whole attitude and outlook upon life will change. Fear of people and of economic insecurity will leave us. We will intuitively know how to handle situations which used to baffle us. We will suddenly realize that God is doing for us what we could not do for ourselves.[4]

The next paragraph upends your remaining wariness:

> Are these extravagant promises? We think not. They are being fulfilled among us—sometimes quickly, sometimes slowly. They will always materialize if we work for them.[5]

Working the Program

The program is not about simply learning the Steps, agreeing to the points they make, and thinking about them. Many who are in Al-Anon and other programs make a distinction between a person who "walks the walk" of the Twelve Steps versus one who only "talks the talk" and sounds good but doesn't actually devote her- or himself to the life they suggest. Walking the walk means that when a Step suggests you make a list, you actually sit down with pencil and paper and write a list. When it suggests that you make a decision, it doesn't mean that you passively comply and move on to the next Step. It means that until *you* have encountered that issue, voiced your disagreement with it, honestly expressed your anger or distrust of it, and made your own decision, you have not done the Step. In fact, these Steps take time, honesty, and courage to fulfill in such an active and authentic manner. You will doubtless repeat them many times to discover and renew their value as you grow in the program.

Working the Steps is a process with its own rhythm. You will find a play between action and rest, giving and receiving, learning and relaxing, structure and nurture. The process of the Steps gives a sense of seasons and renewal that explains why people stay in the program.

A "We" Program

The heart of this recovery program originated one day some fifty-odd years ago when one lonely person was trying desperately not to drink. To help himself, he sought out another alcoholic who desperately needed to hear his story. They each benefitted immensely from that exchange. Their meeting was the start of AA, and a spirit of "we" infuses every part.

People in Twelve Step programs often say this is a "We" program rather than an "I" program. What that means is that the Steps are written with plural pronouns because they describe a group's experience together and assume you will practice them as a group member. It is not possible to work the Steps in an individualized or isolated way.

The first Step doesn't begin with a statement like "First we called a meeting of the group. . . ." The group's existence is not explicitly stated in the Steps, perhaps because the group was so much a part of the founder's experience that it was like the air they breathed. If you tried to do the program by yourself you would miss an essential part of the program and its healing formula: doing the Steps in relationship with other people who need it as much as you do. You can try to live by the principles, but you cannot work this program without active participation with other recovering members at regular meetings.

The Twelve Traditions were written later to guide groups in their organization and to address the "we" aspect more directly than the Steps. The first tradition of Al-Anon states it this way: "Our common welfare should come first; personal progress for the greatest number depends upon unity."[6] It creates a healing, nourishing network of relationships that support and encourage individual growth.

Psychotherapy and the Twelve Steps Are Different Approaches

Many have said that the Twelve Steps are therapy. We don't think of them as therapy, at least not in the traditional sense. Traditional psychotherapy brings change through an uncovering process, whereas the Twelve Step program brings change through something like an apprenticeship in which you join with others to learn how to live a happier life. Psychotherapy emphasizes removing the blocks to your strengths and your true personality. The Twelve Steps give your life a structure that brings you into fellowship with others and teaches you how to grow and live a healthy life.

Many goals of the Twelve Steps and of psychotherapy are similar and the lines between them are blurred. They often work well together, since each approach enhances the other. You can get important guidelines for living from your Twelve Step group that therapy does not emphasize. And you can get important leadership and direction for specific problems in therapy that the Twelve Steps do not provide. The program can be a part of your long-term lifestyle, while therapy can provide a more goal-directed, time-limited effort for your growth.

A Group of Peers

When a group of people with a similar problem get together, they have a special understanding, a bond. This peer group factor is an aspect of the spiritual experience that is closely guarded by two principles in the Traditions. One principle is that the groups meet without charge to anyone. A voluntary collection is taken up to pay the cost of using a room and perhaps to purchase literature or refreshments for the members.

This is a form of help that comes out of a group of peers joining together for mutual benefit. People may come from many different walks of life, varying backgrounds, and financial means, but in their problems and crises they are equals. They are on similar paths to recovery. Some doubters ask, "How can I get help from a bunch of people who have the same problems I have?"

The answer is that there is more than one kind of help. Some kinds come only from people who have the special knowing of common experience; other kinds come only from experts.

The organization is extremely nonauthoritarian and democratic. The traditions state that "our leaders are but trusted servants; they do not govern."[7] Leaders are chosen for brief terms from the membership to convene meetings and serve the needs of the group. No one has authority to tell anyone else what to do. When someone brings a problem or concern to the meeting, no one gives advice. Instead, members listen to each other and they may tell about their own experience with a similar problem. Perhaps they say, "You remind me of the time I felt the way you feel today. When that happened to me, this is what I did. . . ."

Telling Your Story

Language is a unique human trait that brings us nearer to our true selves and joins us in alliances with others as they hear us and we hear them on our similar paths. The healing value of talk is like fresh water and clean air. It may be abundant and easily taken for granted. Psychotherapists know the immense healing effect of telling your own story. In fact, a traditional ritual of Twelve Step meetings is telling your story. The story of your struggles, your mistakes, your good luck and bad, takes you a long, long way toward change and letting your wounds be healed. Hear yourself put your memories and thoughts into words, get the reaction of a friend, and feel the power of such a moment:

> Several times in my meeting I told about my life as it was controlled by alcohol and codependent behavior. I'm always petrified before I talk and always amazed at what I hear myself say when it comes out. Usually one or two others talk first and each one shows me something I hadn't seen before; or when they see something in themselves, I can see it in me too. By the time it's my turn things come out that I didn't know were there at the start. I learn both from what others say and from what comes out of me.

Personal stories shared between people release the pain of your grief, relieve haunting flashbacks, nightmares, and fears of old trauma, and are the only way to resolve relationship problems. Indeed, the back and forth of communication is a bridge between people, for children to develop and for adults to continue their growth. We know that our ancient ancestors told their myths and stories to one another around cooking fires and tribal dances; in those customs lie the origins of civilization. In doing a similar thing in your meeting, you draw from a deep and ancient well of natural resources.

The universe gives me what I need.
The world is a place where happiness is possible.

CHAPTER NINE

TODAY'S MEDITATION: HAPPINESS
In the end,
all that matters is light and dark,
and what's not finished between them.
As long as he stands back far enough, deeply
enough inside the room, he is fine, he gets
the point of things: how they come, then must go.
But the blue sea beyond the window: it has
always done this to him, always forced him
further into happiness than he thought he could stand to go.

—Jim Moore

Becoming Your True Self

This beautiful poem reveals with humility and humor the suggestion that sometimes happiness is difficult for humans to bear. As people continue in their program, they become more able to stand the good things. They begin to see the world as a place where happiness might be possible after all.

Many changes come with recovery; life gets better, richer, yet not easy. Feelings that were once covered up may pop up with startling intensity. People sometimes have trouble accepting the unsettling loss of control that comes with trust.

We'd like to close the book with this chapter, discussing some of the puzzles and challenges along the road: the idea of "progress, not perfection" and the fact of codependency slips. Finally, we'd like to offer a list of the welcome changes that you can expect for yourself and your friends in recovery.

Progress, Not Perfection

If recovery is a journey, and only death is perfection, then nobody on this path has reached a perfect program. How do people handle their own imperfections? Because this is a shaming culture and because many in the program grew up in shaming families, the old tapes of shame may start playing at any moment. It is important to remember stories that affirm the idea of progress, not perfection. An Al-Anon member tells the following story:

In the ten years since I started my program, my life has changed . . . not much on the outside, but inwardly. I have the first sense of what it is to be happy, what it is to be normal. But progress is slow. This summer my old friend from my back-to-the-country days, Jan, came to visit me from the West. She wanted to do the city, and so, like the country mouse and the city mouse, we went sightseeing. One morning, after several days of doing museums and restaurants, I suggested we walk through the bird refuge. She suddenly realized how much she liked the idea: "I really want to see a cardinal. I've never seen one. They don't come to us out West." Well, when she said that, I immediately tensed up. I thought, *How can I produce a cardinal on command?* But I didn't say much. We went out to the park, walked for several miles and enjoyed the cattails, the ducks, the sky. The whole time I was tensed up, worrying about cardinals. We didn't see any birds in the bird refuge.

When we were almost back to the parking lot, I saw or felt a whirring of redness in the peripheral vision of my left eye. Yes, it was a cardinal. It flew straight across our path, at eye level, then perched in a pine tree, to our right, still at eye level. "There's your cardinal," I said. Jan stood silently, she was maybe five feet away from it. The cardinal was a bright red male. He was beautiful. He posed for her, stared at her, cocked his head, and took off.

Then she turned to me and said, "You've been worried I wouldn't get to see a cardinal." I nodded and we both laughed, acknowledging my worry. "So," she said, "you're still thinking you have to fix it, whenever anybody wants anything, the eternal big sister." She knows how it is, because we're on the same journey.

"Yes," I said, "recovery is slow."

"All I said was I wanted to see a cardinal. I didn't ask you to get one for me."

The whirring of the redness stays in my memory: reminding me, I don't have to take care of everything;

reminding me, other people have a higher power; reminding me, the universe gives us not only what we need, but sometimes what we want.

Codependency Slips

We all know that recovering addicts are always vulnerable to slips. They may return to their old addictive "fix" momentarily or permanently.

Codependency slips are less obvious, because they exist more in your mind or in the way you react. For a recovering addict, a slip is an overt act, such as taking a drug or placing a bet. Either it happened or it didn't. But with recovering codependency, you can slip into excessive concern about another person and abandon your personal boundaries through vague and unseen changes. Slips are always possible. We believe your program will be strengthened when you know the potential pitfalls you face.

What is a slip? A codependency slip is a return to old thought and behavior patterns that diminish or defeat you and harm your relationships. Since recovery is a journey, a slip may sidetrack you into a dead-end or a pitfall along the way. For some people, a slip becomes a long-term distraction from personal growth. For others, it may only be temporary if it is identified when it occurs and used as a learning experience.

Recovery follows an up-and-down route; it's like learning how to play golf or do any other skill or craft. One day you learn the best stance and arm motion in swinging the golf club, the next day you advance further in your skill, but perhaps the third day you fall back into your old habits or tendencies. That day you struggle harder and feel frustrated because you don't want to regress. But that day is also an essential stage in your learning because it helps you feel the difference between good and bad golf swings.

Similarly, progress in your recovery never goes in a straight line. In personal growth, there is always a strong inclination to return to the familiar, well-worn paths that you relied upon in the past. Whenever you feel stress, you are more prone to former ways of coping. What you learned in the past about survival in hard times never disappears from your learning, any more so than your skill at riding a bicycle disappears when you don't ride. When your anxiety rises, when you feel the stress of change, the pressure of work to be done, or the threat of an unknown future, you may fall back upon past codependent behaviors, like obsessing:

Carol had an exhausting week at work because her co-worker was on vacation and she had to fill all the orders that two people normally handled. So when she got home on Friday evening she said, "I just want to flop on the couch and vegetate for a while." But her husband was sick with a fever and headache and her daughter needed a ride to a slumber party at a friend's house.

By the time she was able to rest that evening she felt overwhelmed and exhausted. It seemed that life required far more than she could cope with and everything was coming apart. When she lay down to rest, her mind focused on the conversation she had overheard between her daughter and a friend on the telephone. She didn't just wonder about whether her daughter was making a good choice with that friend, she worried that her whole life was headed for catastrophe!

Carol intended to give her husband the loving care he needed while he was sick, but she felt so depleted of energy that she lost track of all she'd learned from Al-Anon about remembering to also take care of herself. So while she brought him his chicken soup she felt like a martyr and a servant. She got overly solicitous about him and developed obsessive thoughts about her daughter's life. In the process she didn't make real contact with either one and felt more anxious and alone. When her daughter came home from the party, Carol was glad to see her but she didn't say that. Instead she lashed out, "I guess life is just one big party for you! There will be no more social life for you until you do your homework and get your room cleaned, young lady!"

When Sunday night came around she went to her Al-Anon meeting and talked about what was happening. Her friends there helped her see that under her stress she had slipped into old codependent coping responses. She was "in survival mode" but not effectively helping herself or anyone else. She needed to regain her emotional detachment from the people she loved and trust the recuperative powers within each of them. She also needed some physical rest to restore her energy.

In Alcoholics Anonymous, *H.A.L.T.* is a commonly used acronym to alert addicts that they are into dangerous territory. It stands for *Hungry, Angry, Lonely, Tired.* Addicts have learned from experience that with each of those feelings they become more vulnerable to a slip. When they have two or three of the feelings at a time they become extremely vulnerable. This is equally true for codependency. Healthy recovery demands good self-care. If one of your basic needs for food, rest, and human closeness goes unfilled, you will be more vulnerable to resorting to old survival methods. It becomes your duty to make sure that you get the basics you need to maintain your strength. Don't deny your needs and say, "I can get along without . . . ," because then you set yourself up for a slip.

Red Flag Warnings
What are some warning signs that you have slipped off the trail?

- Feeling hypercritical toward those around you.
- Your belief that you are more worried about your loved ones than they are about themselves.
- Constantly wondering, *How am I doing?* on the scorecard of another person.
- Repeatedly trying to persuade someone else to take better care of her- or himself.
- Monitoring someone else's addictive behavior or substance use.
- Repeated and willing neglect of your needs for the sake of someone else's (on most occasions).
- Constantly checking with others for signs that they are angry or unhappy and trying to fix everything for them.
- Chronic feelings of guilt or shame: *If something is wrong, it must be my fault.*

- Psychosomatic pains such as headaches, muscle pains, stomach upsets, chronic fatigue.
- Feeling as if you have no choices, you are in a trap, or all of your choices make you feel bad or guilty. "I can't win for losing!" is a typical response.
- "Walking on eggshells" around certain people because you feel there is no room for mistakes.

You may have some of your own particular red-flag signals to add to this list. Perhaps a specific feeling or a behavior with a certain person signals you that you are falling back into old patterns. When you can identify them you are better able to deal with them. Early in recovery, you may recognize that you have slipped only long after you have become immersed in old patterns. But as you become more familiar with the signals you can catch yourself just as you begin to get off the track.

How Do You Get Back on Track?

The first thing to do to get back into your recovery program is to make personal contact with someone else who is a peer on your journey in your Twelve Step group. You might do that at a meeting where you describe what has been happening in your life. Or you might call your sponsor or friend to talk about it. The most important thing is that you learn to stay on your journey, even through stressful times, by telling others about the details of your life. Some people get more support by going to two or three meetings a week for a while instead of just one. If you have a regular evening group, you might also catch a noon meeting during lunch break.

The second thing to do is continue to restore your strength and energy. You need to get enough sleep, good nutrition, plenty of physical exercise, a few minutes for daily peace and quiet or meditation, some relaxation and recreation with friends. Recall what feels good to you. One friend always takes long walks when he feels overwhelmed. Another friend listens to country music when she feels upset.

The Twelve Steps are considered a circle because you keep going around them again and again. If you are concentrating on a particular Step, you are less vulnerable to getting off the trail.

When you find the red flags warning you of a potential slip, select one Step that applies best to you at that time and in your situation. Then dedicate yourself to deepening your practice of its suggestions.

Some Characteristics of Recovering People

This is a list of changes we see in people after a time in recovery. It is not a checklist of positive and negative values. These are some things that recovering people commonly experience:

- a feeling of belonging, of being at peace with the universe and with other people
- living in the moment
- increased ability to feel emotions like love, anger, joy, or grief
- acceptance of your own life history
- greater ability to tell your story to another person
- the ability to act, not just react
- a feeling of contentment with life: *what's given is enough*
- a lessening of the desire to be in control
- a sense of your individual self as distinct from others, and a sense of your life purpose
- freedom and strength to make choices
- less fear when you go out into the world
- the belief that it's okay to show vulnerable feelings
- the ability to set boundaries without a lot of fuss
- affection in relationships
- enjoyment of simple pleasures
- a lessening of physical symptoms
- remission of addictions
- a shift in the way time is perceived: *time is on my side*
- a sense of balance; having a rhythm to your life rather than swinging drastically from one intense moment to the next
- gratitude
- less blame, criticism, negativism, pessimism, shame, and self-pity
- more playfulness
- acceptance of your weaknesses, fears, and incompleteness
- the sense of journey: acceptance of change and forward movement
- trust

You may have other characteristics that you want to add to this list as touchstones for your own journey. In fact, many people gain clarity about their recovery by listing the changes they've seen in their lives after several years on their journey. Change may be gradual. It may be so slow that the only way it can be detected is by looking at daily life five years ago and daily life now, looking at the small details that add up to the cumulative effect of serenity.

The writer Jeanne Shepard has expressed this sense of slow change in a poem she wrote when someone asked her about the major turning points in her life. She sat down to write about the question. Not a single major turning point came to mind—and she had lived many years. So she wrote this poem:

WHAT ARE THE TURNING POINTS THAT CHANGED YOUR LIFE?

Looking back
I've never found
those celebrated
sudden turns,
only slow curves,
light increasing
gradually—
as in the night
when clouds drift
past the moon
and shadows on the grass
shift
and change their shape.

No sudden thunder
with the rising sun—

awakening takes time.

—Jeanne Shepard

Endnotes

Chapter 1: Living for the Eyes of Others

1. Melody Beattie, *Codependent No More* (Center City, Minn.: Hazelden Foundation, 1987), 31.
2. Anne Wilson Schaef, *Co-Dependence: Misunderstood—Mistreated* (Minneapolis: Winston Press, 1986), 21.
3. Wendy Kaminer, "Chances Are You're Codependent Too," *New York Times Book Review*, 11 February 1990.
4. Carol Tavris, "One More Guilt Trip for Women," *Star Tribune*, 3 November 1990, Minneapolis ed., 21A.
5. Virginia Satir, lecture on Family Therapy, St. Paul, June 1985.

Chapter 2: Beginning the Search for Your True Self

1. Herbjørg Wassmo, *The House with the Blind Glass Windows* (Seattle: Seal Press, 1987), 3.
2. Michael E. Kerr and Murray Bowen, *Family Evaluation* (New York: Norton, 1988), 95.
3. Gloria Anzaldua, *Borderlands/La Frontera: The New Mestiza* (San Francisco: Spinsters/Aunt Lute, 1987), 87.
4. Gene Oishi, "To Internees, Reparations Mean More Than Money," *Star Tribune*, Sunday, 21 October 1990, Minneapolis ed.
5. Alice Walker, *The Color Purple* (San Diego: Harcourt, 1982), 176.

Chapter 3: A Light at the End of the Tunnel: Facing Your Problems and Asking for Help

1. Step One of Co-Dependents Anonymous. The entire Twelve Steps of Alcoholics Anonymous, Al-Anon, and Co-Dependents Anonymous appear on pages 127-129 of this book.
2. The text of Alcoholics Anonymous (the Big Book) uses the phrase "God as we understood Him." Considered in the context of the late 1930s, the reference to god as "Him" would not strike anyone as inconsistent with the Step, since the convention was, and still is, to use the masculine pronoun when referring to god. But we believe that replacing the word "Him" with "god" is actually more faithful to the original meaning of the Step. In this

program, no one presumes to define god for anyone else, and that includes assigning gender. For that reason, in the wording of Steps Seven and Eleven we also replace the word "Him" with "god." This is also the version of the Step as Co-Dependents Anonymous states it.

3. Marion Woodman, "Worshiping Illusions," *Parabola* 12 (May 1987): 64.

4. Step One of Alcoholics Anonymous.

5. David Berenson, M.D., "A Systemic View of Spirituality: God and Twelve Step Programs as Resources in Family Therapy." *Journal of Strategic and Systemic Therapies* 9(1)1990: 59-70.

6. Dr. Joseph Sittler, *Spirituality Explored*, a videotape by Video Publishing Co., Filmedia, Inc. (Minneapolis: 1983). Currently available through Seraphim, Inc., St. Paul, Minn.

7. Helen Palmer, *The Enneagram: Understanding Yourself and the Others in Your Life* (San Francisco: Harper & Row, 1988).

8. W. Leadbeater, *The Chakras* (Wheaton, Illinois: Theosophical Publishing House, 1973).

9. Otto Kroeger and Janet M. Thuesen, *Type Talk* (New York: Delacorte Press, 1988).

10. Stephen Foster and Meredith Little, *The Book of the Vision Quest: Personal Transformation in the Wilderness*, rev. ed. (New York: Prentice Hall Press, 1988).

11. *I Ching or Book of Changes*, trans. by Cary F. Baynes and Richard Wilhelm, 3rd ed., Bollingen Series no. 19 (Princeton: Princeton University Press: 1950). See also Carol K. Anthony, *A Guide to the I Ching*, 3rd ed. (Stow, Massachusetts: Anthony Publishing Co., 1988).

Chapter 5: A New Picture Of Reality: Letting Change Happen

1. Matthew Fox, *Original Blessing* (Santa Fe: Bear & Co., 1983), 85.

Chapter 7: Becoming Visible Persons: Living in the Present

1. Step Twelve of Al-Anon.

2. Brenda Schaeffer, *Love Addiction: Help Yourself Out* (Center City, Minn.: Hazelden Foundation, 1986), 3.

3. Tony Hillerman, *Coyote Waits* (New York: Harper & Row, 1990), 143.

4. Pitseolak, *Pitseolak: Pictures Out of My Life* (Seattle: University of Washington Press, 1971).

Chapter 8: Trusting the Mystery of Transformation

1. David Berenson, M.D., "Alcoholics Anonymous: From Surrender to Transformation." *The Family Therapy Networker* 11 (July-August, 1987): 29.

2. *Alcoholics Anonymous,* 3rd ed. (New York: Alcoholics Anonymous World Services, 1976), 569.

3. *Alcoholics Anonymous,* Ibid., 569-70.

4. Ibid., 83-84.

5. Ibid.

6. *Twelve Steps and Twelve Traditions.* (New York: Alcoholics Anonymous World Services, Inc., New York, 1953). See also the later book modeled after it: *Al-Anon's Twelve Steps & Twelve Traditions,* New York: Al-Anon Family Group Headquarters, 1981).

7. Al-Anon's *Twelve Steps & Twelve Traditions,* 93.

THE TWELVE STEPS OF ALCOHOLICS ANONYMOUS*

What follows is the original version of the Twelve Steps. Al-Anon, Co-Dependents Anonymous, and other Twelve Step programs have adapted these Steps for their members.

1. We admitted we were powerless over alcohol—that our lives had become unmanageable.
2. Came to believe that a Power greater than ourselves could restore us to sanity.
3. Made a decision to turn our will and our lives over to the care of God *as we understood Him*.
4. Made a searching and fearless moral inventory of ourselves.
5. Admitted to God, to ourselves, and to another human being the exact nature of our wrongs.
6. Were entirely ready to have God remove all these defects of character.
7. Humbly asked Him to remove our shortcomings.
8. Made a list of all persons we had harmed, and became willing to make amends to them all.
9. Made direct amends to such people wherever possible, except when to do so would injure them or others.
10. Continued to take personal inventory and when we were wrong promptly admitted it.
11. Sought through prayer and meditation to improve our conscious contact with God *as we understood Him*, praying only for knowledge of His will for us and the power to carry that out.
12. Having had a spiritual awakening as the result of these steps, we tried to carry this message to alcoholics, and to practice these principles in all our affairs.

---

*The Twelve Steps of A.A. are taken from *Alcoholics Anonymous*, 3rd ed., published by A.A. World Services, Inc., New York, N.Y., 59-60. Reprinted with permission of A.A. World Services, Inc.

THE TWELVE STEPS OF AL-ANON*

1. We admitted we were powerless over alcohol—that our lives had become unmanageable.
2. Came to believe that a Power greater than ourselves could restore us to sanity.
3. Made a decision to turn our will and our lives over to the care of God *as we understood Him.*
4. Made a searching and fearless moral inventory of ourselves.
5. Admitted to God, to ourselves, and to another human being the exact nature of our wrongs.
6. Were entirely ready to have God remove all these defects of character.
7. Humbly asked Him to remove our shortcomings.
8. Made a list of all persons we had harmed, and became willing to make amends to them all.
9. Made direct amends to such people wherever possible, except when to do so would injure them or others.
10. Continued to take personal inventory and when we were wrong promptly admitted it.
11. Sought through prayer and meditation to improve our conscious contact with God *as we understood Him*, praying only for knowledge of His will for us and the power to carry that out.
12. Having had a spiritual awakening as the result of these steps, we tried to carry this message to others, and to practice these principles in all our affairs.

---

*The Twelve Steps of Al-Anon are adapted from the Twelve Steps of Alcoholics Anonymous and are copyrighted © by Al-Anon Family Group Headquarters, Inc. Reprinted with permission of Al-Anon Family Group Headquarters, Inc., and permission of A.A. World Services, Inc.

THE TWELVE STEPS
OF CO-DEPENDENTS ANONYMOUS*

1. We admitted we were powerless over others—that our lives had become unmanageable.
2. Came to believe that a power greater than ourselves could restore us to sanity.
3. Made a decision to turn our will and our lives over to the care of God as we understood God.
4. Made a searching and fearless moral inventory of ourselves.
5. Admitted to God, to ourselves, and to another human being the exact nature of our wrongs.
6. Were entirely ready to have God remove all these defects of character.
7. Humbly asked God to remove our shortcomings.
8. Made a list of all persons we had harmed, and became willing to make amends to them all.
9. Made direct amends to such people wherever possible, except when to do so would injure them or others.
10. Continued to take personal inventory and when we were wrong promptly admitted it.
11. Sought through prayer and meditation to improve our conscious contact with God as we understood God, praying only for knowledge of God's will for us and the power to carry that out.
12. Having had a spiritual awakening as the result of these steps, we tried to carry this message to other co-dependents, and to practice these principles in all our affairs.

---

*The Twelve Steps of Co-Dependents Anonymous are adapted from the Twelve Steps of Alcoholics Anonymous. Reprinted with permission of A.A. World Services, Inc.